"My Family Doesn't Understand Me!"

Coping Strategies For Entrepreneurs

Yanky Fachler

www.oaktreepress.com

OAK TREE PRESS
19 Rutland Street, Cork, Ireland
www.oaktreepress.com

© 2003 Yanky Fachler

A catalogue record of this book is
available from the British Library.

ISBN 1 86076 268 9

All rights reserved.
No part of this publication may be reproduced
or transmitted in any form or by any means,
including photocopying and recording, without written
permission of the publisher. Such written permission must also
be obtained before any part of this publication is stored in a
retrieval system of any nature.
Requests for permission should be directed to
Oak Tree Press, 19 Rutland Street, Cork, Ireland.

Printed in Ireland by ColourBooks.

CONTENTS

	Introduction	2
Chapter 1	Once Upon a Time, There Were Three Bears ...	5
Chapter 2	On-Tap Family Support — The Myth	9
Chapter 3	Expressions of Hostility	13
Chapter 4	Why Do We Go to School?	25
Chapter 5	Citizens of Planet Ladder	37
Chapter 6	A Planet Where They Speak Entreprenese	45
Chapter 7	Lonely at the Top	55
Chapter 8	Coping Strategies for Entrepreneurs	63
Chapter 9	Bridging the Communication Gap	71
Chapter 10	Coping Strategies for Families	81
Chapter 11	The Three Bears Revisited	91
	About the Author	

Acknowledgements & Dedication

My thanks to the usual suspects for their continued support and friendship. As usual, Gráinne Harte and Alan Clark deserve special thanks for always being there for me. My partner Mona provides me with a constant supply of space, love and belief that continues to sustain me. Finally, thanks to my parents, my sons, my daughters in law, my brothers and sisters, my nieces and nephews, Mona's children, my friends and my colleagues. I thrive on their encouragement.

I dedicate this book to the memory of three dear friends. The late John Furman was a constant source of inspiration for the 15 years I was privileged to know him. I will always value the late Buby Bornstein's lifelong interest in my personal and professional development. And the world is a poorer place without the vivacity of the late Julia Garb, a beautiful human being.

INTRODUCTION

There is no shortage of myths in the "Start Your Own Business" field. These myths, as I have discovered from talking to thousands of people thinking of making the emotional switch from employee to self-employed, can rapidly assume the mantle of accepted wisdom – despite little evidence that they are ever subjected to any real scrutiny.

A common myth is that all entrepreneurs are risk-takers.

The trouble with this sweeping generalisation is that very few people who have actually started their own business define themselves as being drawn to risk. For example, I would never define myself as a risk-taker. I don't gamble. I don't bunjee-jump. It seems that, from the inside looking out, what others may regard as risk is defined by entrepreneurs as simply exploiting a business opportunity.

Another myth is that only people whose parents run a business should themselves become entrepreneurs.

This, too, does not stand the test of reality. Yes, growing up in an entrepreneurial environment can help shape our pro-entrepreneurial attitudes. However, it is too glib to claim that no one whose parents are salaried employees should start their own business.

But of all the "Start Your Own Business" myths out there, one of the most prevalent and widely-held is probably the myth of the universal and dependable availability of emotional support from family.

There seems to be broad consensus among trainers and trainees alike that full support from your family is a pre-condition for starting your own business. There is only one problem with this consensus. On the ground, in the real world of entrepreneurial endeavour, this does not match the experience of most people embarking on the entrepreneurial trail – nor of most their families.

I first aired my thoughts on the issue of family buy-in in my first book, *Fire in the Belly: An Exploration of the Entrepreneurial Spirit* (Oak Tree Press, 2001):

You will be unpleasantly surprised to discover that not everyone is as supportive of your decision to become an entrepreneur and open your own business as you expected.

"You call that a real job?" is the sort of comment you may have to endure (from spouses, parents, friends and even children). "How could you be so irresponsible?"

The sad and often cruel truth is that on-tap family support for would-be entrepreneurs is the exception, not the rule. In fact, automatic family support is a myth.

I expanded on this theme in articles published in the business press (*Business Plus, Smart Moves* e-zine). But I always felt that there was a book waiting to be written.

The catalyst was an invitation to address the Association for Enterprise Opportunity (AEO) annual conference in Fort Lauderdale, Florida. I proposed the family support myth as my theme and the organisers were quick to inform me that, since no one had ever discussed this topic before in their conferences, they were including me in the seminar schedule.

May 2002 found me in the illustrious company of my Oak Tree Press colleagues Brian O'Kane and Ron Immink, as part of the cosmopolitan

Irish contingent (Brian from Cork, Ireland *via* Calcutta, India; Ron from the Netherlands; and me from England *via* Israel) at the Florida event. Ron attended my advanced workshop for practitioners, "Why Families Can't Give Emotional Support". During the Q&A session, there was a torrent of verbal fireworks as participants argued the pros and cons of the issues raised.

News of the furore spread among the conference participants, and even people who had not attended the seminar were eager to debate the issue hotly with me. At a certain point in the proceedings, my Oak Tree Press colleagues cornered me and delivered their two-word demand: "Start writing!".

This book is the result of that gentle request.

Yanky Fachler
Dundalk
March 2003

Chapter 1
Once Upon a Time There Were Three Bears...

I f you are sitting comfortably, I would like to tell you a story ...

Once upon a time, in a place called Honeytown, there lived three bears: Mummy Bear, Daddy Bear and Baby Bear.

Mummy Bear was a supervisor at the Honeytown Glass Jar Company.

Daddy Bear worked as a security guard in the local branch of First National Honey Bank.

Baby Bear was minded by Grandma Bear.

Daddy Bear was very good at his job, and frequently made suggestions to management on how they could tighten up security at the bank.

But from an early age, Daddy Bear always had a bee in his bonnet. An entrepreneurial bee. He had always liked the idea of being his own boss, and kept a constant eye open for a suitable opportunity.

One day as he was browsing through the Honeytown Times, *he read a report that Bruinbank, Paddington Bank and Rupert Bank had all announced plans to open branches in Honeytown within the next few months.*

"This is my chance", thought Daddy Bear. "I can use my expertise and my experience to set up my own bank security consultancy business that will offer its services to the new banks coming into town".

Bursting with excitement and energy, Daddy Bear went bouncing home to share his good news with Mummy Bear.

"Guess what, honeybunch," he told her. "I've decided to leave my job in the bank, and to become my own boss. I'm going to start my own business as a bank security consultant".

Mummy Bear rushed up to Daddy Bear and almost knocked him over with the force of her loving bear hug.

"Oh sweetie", she said. "You're my hero. You're so brave. I always knew you had it in you. I always dreamed that I'd marry someone with drive, someone with ambition, someone who knew how to take the initiative. Baby Bear will be so proud to have a daddy who runs his own business".

"And of course, sweetie," Mummy Bear murmured into his ear, "you know you can always count on me for all the emotional support you need, you clever Daddy Bear, you".

That evening, Mummy Bear organised an impromptu get-together for all the family to tell them about Daddy Bear's plans. Grandpa Bear slapped Daddy Bear on the back as he growled: "Good for you, son". Daddy Bear's brother Bruno heartily congratulated him, and Cousin Beryl Bear slapped a great big kiss on Daddy Bear's cheek.

Delighted, validated and empowered by the enthusiastic response of Mummy Bear and the other members of the Bear family, Daddy Bear gave in his notice at Honeytown Bank.

He set up his own bank security business, and was soon running a successful company supplying security services to all the banks in Honeytown and beyond.

Daddy Bear, Mummy Bear and Baby Bear all lived happily ever after.

The End.

Chapter 2
On-Tap Family Support: The Myth

If you like fairy tales, I'm sure you enjoyed the story of the Three Bears. I'm sure it gave you a warm and cuddly feeling. If you *really* like reading fairy tales with a happy end, you will find plenty more stories like this in any decent bookshop or library.

And if you think I am directing you to the Children's Section, I'm not.

If you like fairy stories, you should make a beeline for the Business Section. When you get there, take a look at the shelves that heave with a huge choice of "How To Start Your Own Business" titles.

As you browse through the books, you'll find that they divide into three broad categories. The first consists of those "How To" books that make no significant mention of family support.

The second category includes a small number of titles that warn you that family support cannot be taken for granted. An excellent book in this category is **Honey, I Want To Start My Own Business**, by Azriella Jaffe (HarperBusiness, 1997). But even this author focuses on the challenges facing the supportive spouse, even if that spouse is having a hard time giving that support.

The vast majority of "Start Your Own Business" titles, however, belongs to the third category. This is the category that spins you a fairy tale remarkably similar to the Three Bears story. The books in this category present a twin-pronged view of family support:

- Emotional support from your family is critical to the success of your enterprise.
- Emotional support from your family is universally and dependably available.

Such sentiments are not confined only to bookshops and libraries. Most "Start Your Own Business" courses, and most of the thousands of websites devoted to entrepreneurship, also emphasise the critical nature of family support.

Here are just a few examples of what you will find in many books, magazines and websites:

You need the support of your family.

Your family members and other individuals who depend on you must wholeheartedly support your endeavour.

Don't go walking out onto that start-up tightrope without the support of loved ones to steer you in the right direction.

While family and friends may not be able to relate to your specific fears about starting a business, you should be able to count on them for emotional support.

Families will have to understand that the home atmosphere should be very supportive. With a family, deciding to found an enterprise is likely to be more successful as a family decision.

The budding entrepreneur must have the full support of their family. Without their backing, you are not firing on all pistons.

Unless you can honestly tell yourself that you will get help and support from your family, it would be wise to review the situation.

A prime example of this approach appeared on a panel at the stand of a national enterprise agency in a major Enterprise Show:

> *Indeed, we'd go so far as to say that you shouldn't even consider the possibility of starting a business unless your family wholeheartedly supports your decision to start a business.*

According to this broad consensus, unless you have the support of your family, you are better off forgetting and foregoing any notion of starting your own business. This message is repeated in countless books, articles, websites and training courses: If you cannot count on family for emotional support, your entrepreneurial venture is likely to run into trouble.

The consensus about family support spreads beyond just the professional literature. In certain US cities, people applying for microenterprise funding discover that some funding organisations are so wedded to the concept of family support that they even demand written proof of this from the potential entrepreneur's family before they are prepared to lend money to start a new business.

So why do I have a problem with the consensus that assumes the on-tap availability of family support? Is it because I believe that family support is not important or of no value? Of course not. We all need family.

> *Call it a clan, call it a network, call it a tribe, call it a family. Whatever you call it, whoever you are, you need one. (Jane Howard).*

> *One's family is the most important thing in life. I look at it this way: One of these days I'll be over in a hospital somewhere with four walls around me. And the only people who'll be with me will be my family. (US Senator Robert C. Byrd)*

> *The family seems to have two predominant functions: to provide warmth and love in time of need and to drive each other insane. (Donald G Smith)*

Of course entrepreneurs would love to receive emotional support from their families. Family support is a wonderful ideal – **if** you can get it.

The problem lies in the fact that we rarely receive the on-tap family support we want. As generations of people who have announced their intention of becoming their own boss will attest, would-be entrepreneurs receive everything but family support.

That is why for most people, the level of family support displayed by Mummy Bear in our story is wishful thinking at best, and a dangerous myth at worst.

Why do I call it dangerous? Because it creates false hopes and generates false expectations.

Why do I call it a myth? Because most of our loved ones are incapable of delivering the level of emotional support that entrepreneurs want.

If we encourage entrepreneurs to believe that they can automatically expect emotional support from their family, we are sending out the wrong message. We are doing entrepreneurs a great disservice if we insist that no one should even think of starting their own business without family support. Unless we furnish entrepreneurs with tools to handle adverse reactions from their families, we are guilty of misleading them.

In this book, we will challenge the myth of on-tap family support, and we will offer a suite of coping strategies for the real world of "Start Your Own Business", a world where entrepreneurs are more likely to meet hostility than encouragement.

Chapter 3
Expressions of Hostility

If the story of the Three Bears is indeed a myth and a fairy tale, what is the reality?

Let us pick up the story where Daddy Bear comes bouncing home to share his good news. (Of course, it doesn't have to be Daddy Bear. It could just as easily be Mummy Bear bursting with enthusiasm to announce *her* entrepreneurial intentions to Daddy Bear).

There is one important respect in which our Three Bears story got it right. The entrepreneurial announcement never fails to elicit a reaction.

And that reaction is rarely a neutral reaction. For example, it would be hard to imagine the following scenario:

Daddy Bear: *Guess what, honeybunch, I've decided to be my own boss.*

Mummy Bear: *How nice. Yes dear, that's very interesting.*

Mummy Bear's reaction is unlikely to be so insipid.

But it is equally unlikely that she will meet Daddy Bear's entrepreneurial announcement with the unmitigated glee she displayed in our story.

Before we examine family reactions in the real world, let us fantasise for a moment. Let's imagine that we are in Daddy Bear's shoes. Let's imagine that we are about to share with our family (spouse, significant other, parents, children, best friends and other family members) the good news that we intend to start our own business.

What sort of response would we really like to receive? What ideal script would we write for this scene?

I'm sure that in this script, we would all love to be praised to the heavens for our drive, ambition and initiative. We would all love to be congratulated. We would all love to receive the best wishes of our family. In short, we would all love to receive the emotional bear hug like the one Mummy Bear gave Daddy Bear.

Which makes the reaction we receive in the real world all the more difficult to comprehend. Because when we look beyond the platitudes and wishful thinking, when we examine the experience of real people in real families, a very different picture emerges.

Instead of praise and congratulations, we are far more likely to hear abuse, disappointment and downright hostility.

Over the years, I have asked thousands of people in my "Start Your Own Business" seminars to share their experiences of what really transpired when they made their entrepreneurial announcement to the family. Most of them have sad tales to tell.

Based on their feedback, I have divided the negative reactions received from family into four broad categories:

- Questioning our mental health
- Outrage
- Put-down
- Threat/ultimatum.

Questioning Our Mental Health

In the first category of negative reactions, the family members greet our entrepreneurial announcement by trying to question our mental health:

- Are you mad?
- You've gone soft in the head.
- Have you lost it?
- You're crazy.
- You're out of your mind.
- You're behaving foolishly.
- You need your head examined.
- You need a psychiatrist.
- You're acting in an unstable manner.
- You're having a nervous breakdown (or the Jewish/Irish/Polish Mother equivalent: "You're giving me a nervous breakdown.")

CASE STUDY

Every year, I am invited to give a seminar to the mature students in the Careers Centre of the San Diego Regional College in California. One year, my audience consisted of over 50 web design students at the college who were all toying with the idea of become freelance web designers.

In the course of the seminar, I expressed my view that family buy-in is a myth. I told the audience that, in reality, most aspiring entrepreneurs are greeted with very negative feedback instead of support and encouragement.

There was a general nodding of heads, a buzz of recognition, and after a few minutes we moved on to another aspect of starting your own business.

At the end of the evening, a 40-something participant came up to me and thanked me profusely.

"You're welcome", I replied.

"No, you don't understand", she said.

"I'm thanking you because you have lifted a heavy weight from my shoulders. I first announced my intention of becoming a freelance web designer to my family two years ago. Their reaction was terrible. All my family and all my friends started treating me as if I'd gone funny in the head.

"Tonight I learned that I am normal, and that they are the ones who don't get it. Tonight is the first time in two years that I don't feel like a freak. I am thanking you for liberating me."

Outrage

The second category of negative reactions that we are likely to receive from family is outrage:

- How dare you!
- You've got some nerve!
- What's got into you?
- That's preposterous!
- You arrogant bastard!
- How can you be so irresponsible?
- Who do you think you are!
- What about the mortgage?
- What about the children's education?
- What about our European vacation?

Case Study

Jody and Rob inherited a very large house, and one of the first urgent tasks was to have the carpets cleaned. When Jody called the carpet cleaning companies she found in her local classified telephone directory, she was shocked at the prices they were demanding. She and Rob were both salaried employees, and simply could not afford such prices.

Jody decided to clean the carpets herself, and found a machine hire company where she could hire a huge industrial-size cleaner. She had a ball cleaning her carpets, and everyone who visited her house remarked on how clean the carpets were. Some visitors even thought that the carpets had been newly laid. Friends were soon asking Jody to clean their carpets, and she was to be found most weekends in her friends' homes with the industrial cleaner that she hired each time.

It did not take long for Jody to realise that she was having much more fun cleaning carpets than working in her boring office job. She decided that she wanted to get into carpet cleaning full-time, and rushed back home to inform Rob that she was giving up her salaried job and setting up her own carpet cleaning business. His response was not exactly what Jody expected:

"How can you be so f...ing selfish!" he exploded.

Jody was shocked.

As she told the other participants in my seminar: "I couldn't believe it. Here was the man I loved, the father of our three children, and the best response he could come up with when I announced my exciting decision was that I was selfish!"

This particular story actually has a happy end. Undeterred by Rob's hostile attitude, Jody went ahead anyway. She bought her own industrial cleaner, and demand for her carpet cleaning services grew and grew.

Within a year, Rob saw that his "selfish" wife was earning more than he was — so he quit his job and became the sales manager of her company.

Put-down

The third category of negative reactions is the put-down:

- Stop kidding yourself.
- Get real.
- You'll never make it.
- How could you be so stupid?
- What a dumb idea.
- Stop dreaming.
- Typical of you to think only of yourself.
- Why are you so stubborn?
- Is this another bee in your bonnet?
- You don't have what it takes to be your own boss.

CASE STUDY

After 20 years with the same employer, Jack was miserable. He didn't like his colleagues at the appliance maintenance centre where he worked. He didn't like his bosses. He didn't like having to field calls all day from irate customers complaining about the shoddy service. In fact, Jack didn't really like being an employee. In the back of his mind, he had always harboured fantasies of going out on his own.

Jack's opportunity came when he learned that the elderly proprietor of the computer repair workshop where he used to take his second-hand laptop for servicing was planning to retire. Jack had always enjoyed tinkering with computers, and he believed that, with some extra training, he could make a go of the business. He negotiated terms with the owner, and decided that it was now time to share his plans with his wife, Maggie.

Jack had not given too much thought to Maggie's reaction. He assumed that, once she saw the wisdom of his moving into a field that he liked instead of suffering in his current place of work, she would give the idea the thumbs up.

But, instead of encouraging Jack to follow his star, she threw a fit.

"If you failed in such an easy job as the one you have now, how do you think you'll succeed in a job that requires much more intelligence, experience and expertise? Who do you think is going to bail you out when your fall flat on your face? And I'll tell you something else, don't think you can come knocking on my door when your enterprise fails."

Jack was devastated. The ferocity of Maggie's tirade caught him unprepared. She had successfully poured cold water on all his enthusiasm and all his plans.

Unwilling to stand up to Maggie's onslaught, Jack chose the path of least resistance. He never did start his own business, and remained a thoroughly disgruntled employee for the remainder of his working life.

Threat / Ultimatum

The final category of negative reactions is the threat or ultimatum:

- Over my dead body.
- No way.
- That's what you think.
- If you go ahead, I'm outta here.
- Read my lips – No, you're not.
- I categorically forbid you to do this.

CASE STUDY

In May 2002, I gave a workshop at the Association for Enterprise Opportunity (AEO) Annual Conference in Fort Lauderdale, Florida. The theme of the conference was "Microenterprise: An Ocean of Opportunity", and it was here that I gave my first outing to the "Why families can't give emotional support" seminar on which this book is based.

The subject of family support is a highly emotive issue. In the lively Q&A session after my address, one of the participants took me to task, claiming that I was whitewashing the issue.

"You are not painting a stark enough picture of the negative responses," she said.

She went on to say that, among some of the highly-marginalised women whom she works with in Washington, the decision to try and break the no-hope cycle of poverty and disadvantage by trying to start a small business can sometimes be literally a life and death situation.

"I have had clients who have been badly beaten up by their partners for having the nerve to even raise the possibility that they might start their own microenterprise," she told us.

As we can see from this litany of negative responses, the praise and encouragement that we expect if we believe the myth of on-tap family support are in short supply. Instead, we find our families questioning our mental health, expressing outrage, putting us down and threatening us.

When we hatch entrepreneurial plans, we assume that we will automatically receive support from our families. By failing to factor in the possibility of negative reaction, we are in for an unpleasant surprise.

Most of us are deeply shocked at the wave of negativity we encounter. Many of us start believing that our problem with our family's reaction is our own private secret.

Some of us even believe that we are somehow to blame for the lack of support we receive from our family.

If only I had handled things differently, if only I had said the right thing, my loved ones would have reacted differently.

I see this in my seminars. When we start discussing the difficulties that families have in giving emotional support, the participants start throwing sheepish looks at their colleagues. Eventually, one of the participants usually says something like: "What, you too? I thought it was something wrong with me."

It can be a great relief to discover that most people entering "Start Your Own Business" mode are in the same boat as countless others who have also experienced negative reactions from family.

I recently came across the saying: "You can't say the wrong thing to the right person, and you can't say the right thing to the wrong person".

I think this is very apt. If your family is receptive to your entrepreneurial announcement, they will back you no matter how clumsily you deliver the announcement. And if they are not predisposed to support your entrepreneurial efforts, the most articulate exposition of your plans will not sway them.

I want to repeat that family hostility is not axiomatic. Plenty of people who have started their own business will proudly proclaim how much support they have received from their spouses or significant others. Anyone who has received the whole-hearted support from these unsung heroes and heroines knows that it is something to value, something precious – the more so when they can see how other entrepreneurs have to put up with much less support.

If you do receive emotional support, you deserve sincerest congratulations – as do those who support you.

But the experience of countless entrepreneurs points to a very different reality, a reality where family backing is the exception, not the rule.

A survey conducted in 2002 by accountants Ernst & Young and the London School of Economics quoted one entrepreneur as saying that his family basically wrote him off when he wanted to start his own business. They said his venture would never work. They said that, since he had received so much education, he should use it by working in a merchant bank.

(Incidentally, this was similar to the advice I received from several members of my own family when I first indicated that I wanted to go out on my own: "Why can't you go and get a solid career working in a bank like other normal people?")

In the face of the hostile reception that entrepreneurs receive, we need to ask two questions:

1. What is it that prevents families from delivering the level of support that their entrepreneurial loved ones expect and crave?
2. What can entrepreneurs do about it?

Our focus in the following chapters is to explore why there is such a gaping chasm between what we want to hear and what we actually hear when we announce our decision to follow our own entrepreneurial star.

In the later chapters, our focus will be on real-world coping strategies.

Chapter 4
Why Do We Go to School?

The knee-jerk expressions of hostility within the family to the announcement of entrepreneurial initiative follow such a predictable pattern that they must be part of our upbringing.

If we want clues on how and why we grow up with such negative attitudes to the notion of starting a new business, we would do well to take a close look at our schools. If we want a better idea of why our families go into such a tailspin, we should look at the role of schools and higher learning institutions in shaping our attitudes to self-employment.

One way of monitoring these attitudes is to ask a simple question: Why *do* we go to school?

Whenever I ask my entrepreneurial seminars or school audiences to answer this question, the initial responses are predictable.

"To get an education."

"To learn values."

"To learn social skills."

"To learn communication skills."

"To keep us mentally and physically alert."

The responses of schoolchildren tend to be more honest:

"To play football."

"To have fun".

"We go to school because our parents force us to."

But when we strip away the clichés and shift the focus to the ultimate role of the school system, we discover that people have a very clear idea of the ultimate purpose of education and the ultimate reason for seeking qualifications. The answers are now more grounded:

"To help us get a job."

"To gear us for the job market."

"To make us employable."

I believe that this is the crux of the matter, the key to understanding the way families view self-employment.

Without wanting to sound like a conspiracy theorist, I have a theory that modern Western-style societies forge a sort of secret pact with their respective educational systems.

As part of this pact, society makes schools an offer they cannot refuse. The deal goes something like this:

We will pay you to take our kids off our hands for the next dozen years or so. During that period, you can do what you like with them. You can educate them, you can teach them life skills, and you can broaden their horizons. But above all, you must always remember that the ultimate reason that we entrust you with our children is for you to make sure that they emerge from their educational experience as useful members of society. And in case there is any misunderstanding as to how we define useful members of society, your role is to produce people with the skills needed to become successful employees. To summarise our deal: We fund you. You deliver the workforce.

This pact between society and the schools is highly functional. In exchange for funding, schools undertake to train us to become productive employees. Society is guaranteed a steady flow of people ready to fill job openings in manufacturing, retailing, service industries, academia, public service, and other work sectors.

And although this pact initially involves just the two parties, society and the educational system, plenty of other parties are clamouring to get into the act.

Who are these other parties?

They include:

- Our teachers (who benefit from secure, well-paid jobs).
- Our parents (who, as every teenager knows, are a pillar of the establishment, of society).
- Our church organisations.
- Our political establishment.
- Our community organisations.
- Our business community.

In the belief that employment should be our ultimate goal, all these parties sing lustily from the same song sheet. And the chorus is:

- You study in order to become employable.
- Becoming employable is the main justification for seeking and gaining academic or professional qualifications.
- Education is your passport to the world of employment.

I find it useful to illustrate this pact by thinking of school as a sausage-processing plant.

Imagine a plank (as in a pirate ship plank) poised above a huge pot. As young boys and girls starting out on our school career, we walk this plank and drop off the end into the pot. For the next dozen years, we undergo rigorous processing inside the pot.

All the machinery in this processing plant (the school) and all the machinery operators (the teachers) are geared to ensure that we duly emerge at the end of our school days as educated sausages, waiting to be devoured by the eagerly awaiting job market.

Usually, those of us with more education will take higher level jobs. Those of us with less education will probably take lower level jobs.

But we have one thing in common: we all take jobs.

And what do our parents and extended families think about all this?

They are delighted. They are cheering from the sidelines. They willingly collude in upholding the pact between society and schools.

Parents regard educational and academic prowess as the single most reliable barometer for judging our progress in life as measured by the type of job we secure.

Have you noticed that we ask youngsters "How are you doing at school?" much more often than we ask them "How do you like school?". We are less interested in whether a child is stimulated by the educational experience, and more interested in whether the child is on the right track to eventual employability.

Yet we know that lots of youngsters in the school system will tell you that they are doing well at school, but they are not enjoying the experience.

Why does the initial sense of discovery and invention that characterises the early years at school start to fade when we turn 8, 9 or 10?

I believe it is partly because at this stage, we start realising that school is no more than the sausage-processing plant described above. Children cannot define what is happening, but they sense that they have entered a phase that is less fun, less creative, and more drudge.

Most of us know exactly what our parents mean when they urge us to do well at school. They want us to buy into the societal norm that gaining qualifications is our passport to finding a good job in the employment market.

We also catch on very early what our schools and parents mean when they urge us to get a good job:

- They mean a secure job.
- A job with career prospects.
- A job with a pension.

That is society's definition of a good job, and the only way to get a good job is to go and work for someone else. And, if you *really* want to fulfil society's ideal, then go and work for a large and safe organisation.

It is interesting to see how closely society links school achievement and jobs. If someone does not succeed in the employment world, the blame is invariably placed on lack of achievement in school.

Working for someone else is what we are educated to do, and this is the path we invariably follow. Employable sausages of the world unite!

I know that I have deliberately oversimplified the picture. I know that not all schools are totally and exclusively locked into this mindset. But I have yet to hear of a school principal who openly challenges the role of schools in producing fodder for the employment market.

I can already hear objections that I am ignoring the many schools that have instituted enterprise programmes. After all, these programmes are ostensibly aimed at giving the younger generation a better understanding of the world of enterprise.

In my experience, many school enterprise schemes are characterised more by their promotion of business values than by their promotion of entrepreneurial values.

The two are not synonymous.

Business values prepare us for even better jobs in hierarchical organisations. Business values help to shape us into more valuable sausages.

Entrepreneurial values prepare us for working for ourselves. Entrepreneurial values help to shape us into potential entrepreneurs.

Many schools eagerly embrace business values. Very few schools promote entrepreneurial values.

Much media attention has been focused on the Glasgow, Scotland school where 5-year-olds were given lessons in how to run their own company. By age 6, they were already in business. The children made cakes, which they sold to teachers and classmates. When certain children did not perform well enough and failed to meet their sales or production targets, they were replaced.

The head teacher claimed that her pupils were not too young to be learning how to make money. She said that, by encouraging children to run their own firm at the earliest possible age, "they would grow up with a more positive attitude to business and business success".

Precisely. Business values, not entrepreneurial values. I am sure that these children will indeed grow up with a more positive attitude to business. But I am not convinced that they are really being encouraged to contemplate an entrepreneurial career when they are older.

Semantics are probably to blame for the confusion. The term "entrepreneur" is used too loosely. Maybe we should encourage the school enterprise schemes with awards such as "Best Young Entrepreneur in the School", "Best Young Entrepreneur in the County", "Best Young Entrepreneur in the Country" and "Best Young Entrepreneur in Europe" to re-examine their wording.

A genuine entrepreneurship programme would foster a genuine understanding of the entrepreneurial process. Such programmes would see their primary aim as encouraging youngsters to espouse entrepreneurial values, to adopt an entrepreneurial mindset, to benefit from the element of choice that underpins the entrepreneurial experience.

Most existing school enterprise programmes are more concerned with teaching a good grasp of business values. These schemes simply reinforce the society-school pact, whereby youngsters are taught to become useful members of the employment world.

Case Study

I recently attended a national awards ceremony for a "Young Manager of the Year" scheme. The winners of the seven categories, all aged 16-17, each gave a short speech in which they thanked their teachers, their parents and the school. They also each spoke about their experiences as they worked on their award-winning projects.

Only two of the winners (who had established a microenterprise together) stated categorically that their experience had given them the "fire in the belly" to start their own business.

Three of the seven winners restricted their comments to bland generalisations.

The remaining two winners said that, while they enjoyed the experience, they would never themselves be tempted to take the difficult self-employment route, because they knew that it involved too much hard work.

Now, maybe I am expecting too much, but I could not help wondering why these individuals had been rewarded. It occurred to me that they had been coached in the art of finding a killer enterprise idea and/or execution that would knock the socks off the judges. All the participants also learned valuable lessons about management. But it seems as if any appreciation of the true entrepreneurial aspects of the experience was individual, not structural.

The failure, reluctance or refusal of schools to prepare us properly for any alternative to the world of employment is also reflected in career counselling. I sometimes wonder whether the career guidance advisers and teachers, who dish out career advice so liberally, realise just what an awesome responsibility they carry.

I believe that the whole point of education should be to encourage youngsters to explore the vast array of options that the adult world offers. All too often, however, the people who provide career advice have precious little experience of these options themselves.

The result: youngsters are steered towards easily pigeon-holed career options.

There are three categories of advice recipients:

- There are those who are lucky enough to receive useful and valuable advice. In later years, they look back with gratitude at the adult(s) who helped steer them in the direction they went on to adopt. And, even if they do not act upon this advice, they are thankful for it.
- There are those who do not want advice, who don't listen to advice, and who don't follow advice.
- And then there are the many of us who belong to the third category – those who receive bad advice and, not knowing how bad it really is, go on to follow this bad advice. Misguided negative feedback can cause serious long-term damage. It can dent our self-confidence, undermine our self-image, and shatter our dreams.

CASE STUDY

When Sir Anthony Sher was a young unknown actor, freshly arrived in London from his native South Africa, he somehow managed to get an audition at RADA, the Royal Academy of Dramatic Arts. Although he was very nervous and chose a particularly unsuitable audition piece, he was not prepared for the letter he received from them some weeks later (a letter that he has kept to this day.)

> Not content with informing Sher that he had failed his audition for a place in this prestigious drama school, the writer of the rejection letter also took it upon him or herself to share some advice with Sher:
>
> > *"Not only have you failed, and you must not try again, but we most seriously urge you to think of a different career."*
>
> Lucky for us, Sher ignored this disastrous advice, and turned out to be one of the most gifted actors of his generation. If he had listened to this advice arrogantly printed on RADA notepaper, the world would have been robbed of an amazing talent.

I belonged solidly in the third category. Before I left school, two of my teachers whose opinions I respected felt the need to give me some unsolicited career advice.

One of them told me that I shouldn't set my sights too high, that I should "settle for being a good B", as he put it.

The other teacher told me to avoid anything which involved writing, on the grounds that I lacked imagination.

Because I was a good (as in well-behaved and polite) pupil, and because I believed that my teachers could only have my best intentions in mind, I accepted all too readily their definition of my future. I had already determined to seek the safety and security of paid employment, and their advice only served to reinforce this determination. I told myself that, if my teachers could not discern that I possessed any remarkable talents, they were probably right. Based on their conclusions, I never considered doing anything other than becoming a well-educated sausage working for someone else.

It was not until 15 years later, after I had neutralised the negative self-image that I had absorbed from my two teachers, that I was able to break out of the employment world strait-jacket and embark on an international career as a freelance writer.

Do teachers carry total responsibility for dishing out questionable advice?

No. I acknowledge my own role in what happened to me. It takes two to tango. Had I been in a different category of advice recipients, I would have reacted differently. I know plenty of people who, had they been faced with this kind of advice, would have dismissed it and got on with their lives.

We saw earlier that, in order to fulfil society's ideal, we need to go and work for a large and safe organisation. This is not a criticism. For many of us, the "get a safe job" message we receive at school works for us. Not everyone is suited to start their own business, and it makes no sense to push anyone to take the entrepreneurial route if this is not their own free choice.

But, by the same token, I maintain that not everyone is suited to becoming an employee. Given the number of people who eventually start their own business, statistically there have to be several potential entrepreneurs in every classroom. Although we might not be able to pinpoint them at an early age and, although they often cannot identify themselves, we know that a handful will one day become their own boss.

Actually, sometimes it **is** possible to spot them early. They are the rebels. They are the individualists in the class who are branded by their teachers as non-conformist troublemakers. We know from autobiographies, articles and anecdotal evidence that many people who started their own successful entrepreneurial business were always getting into trouble at school for being different, inattentive, disruptive.

And how does the school system deal with these rebels? Does it encourage kids who display a fertile imagination?

No. The school system tries to stamp on their individuality. After all, they are sausages, and they should know their place.

Case Study

I was invited to address a bunch of 16-year-olds who were receiving their certificates after completing a regional school enterprise programme. The youngsters were accompanied by some of their teachers.

Before I started my address, I told my young audience to ignore the presence of their teachers. I wanted them to feel free to interrupt me, to challenge me, to ask questions, and to stop me if anything I said was not making sense.

At a certain point, I invited them to call out answers to the question I posed at the beginning of this chapter: "Why do we go to school?" With my back to them, I started writing down their answers on the flip-chart.

One particularly alert young lady supplied the following answers:

"If we don't go to school, the authorities could prosecute our parents."

"We go to school to annoy our teachers."

As I was writing down these responses, behind my back I distinctly heard one of the teachers hissing to the pupil: "Stop giving cheeky answers".

I gently reminded the teacher that I had specifically asked the youngsters to be honest and to be open. After my address, the same young lady who had given such spirited answers enquired where she could obtain a copy of my book, **Fire in the Belly**.

I am pretty certain that this precocious girl has all the ingredients for running her own business at some stage in her life. Yet her very precociousness and individuality were already getting her into trouble at school.

Why do teachers so eagerly embrace the pact between society and schools? Why do so few teachers actively encourage the entrepreneurial route?

We needn't look too far for the answer. Remember, teachers are themselves the ultimate product of the school system. Teachers grow up believing that the sensible, normal and advisable route in life is to become an employee. By becoming teachers, they become prime examples of the world of paid employment.

I have no beef with teachers. I am not trying to get at them, and I do not wish to portray teachers as the bad guys. I have had the privilege of meeting and working with exceptional, inspiring and gifted teachers who truly encourage their students to choose their own individual path in life, and who inculcate entrepreneurial values into their classes.

But this does not detract from the fact that the teachers whom schoolchildren encounter every day in the sausage-processing plants that are our schools are living proof that educated sausages can and do go on to get paid jobs. Yesterday's sausages are today's teachers. This is not a criticism, it is an empirical observation.

In this chapter, we explored the way in which we are conditioned to believe that becoming part of the adult world means going out and working for someone else.

We saw that society demands of our schools: "Prepare our kids for the job market".

We saw how everyone buys into this pact between society and the school system.

In the next chapter, we will see how this universal buy-in impacts on our adult lives, and how it impacts on our evolving attitudes towards entrepreneurs.

Chapter 5
On Becoming a Citizen of Planet Ladder

Thanks to the pact between society and schools, most of us emerge from the sausage-processing plant as sausages waiting to be slotted into the job market.

We leave school or college in the knowledge that, sooner or later, we are fated to start our working lives as employees.

Clutching our qualifications (school leaving certificate, university degree, diploma, or whatever), we apply for an opening in the employment market. We embellish our CVs, we send them out to prospective employers, and eventually most of us are rewarded with a job offer. We conduct an inner dialogue with ourselves:

Wow, here is proof that the system really works. Someone is actually prepared to pay us for our efforts. It's just like our parents and our teachers always said: If we go to school, if we study hard and get our qualifications, we will emerge from the sausage processing plant into the eagerly waiting arms of the employment market. And to prove it, society is rewarding us by offering us a job. I really am an employable sausage.

Thus begins our life on the career ladder.

I began introducing the ladder metaphor in my very first "Start Your Own Business" seminars. It was soon clear that participants were starting to use ladder terminology in their questions and comments. They would talk about "ladder people", "non-ladder people", "the ladder world."

This is what gave me the idea to illustrate my talks with a real ladder. Ever since then, whenever I am invited to address a "Start Your Own Business" seminar, workshop, conference, enterprise show or training event, I use a step-ladder to illustrate the ladder/employment idiom. (This often causes some confusion in whatever venue I am using – a hotel, library, conference centre or school. When the maintenance staff find a step-ladder standing in the middle of the room just before the guest lecturer is due to speak, they assume it's there by mistake, and try to remove it. I am forever chasing after my ladders!)

Turning up for work on the very first day in our very first job is an experience we never forget. We're usually feeling quite proud of ourselves as we take that first tentative step over the threshold of the office, shop, plant or other place of employment. All our years in the school system can be seen as preparation and training for this precious moment.

When describing this sense of a lengthy process coming to fruition, I step on to the lowest rung of the ladder and proclaim:

I am now a citizen of Planet Ladder.

The school system encouraged us to subscribe to the goals, rules and regulations of Planet Ladder. We were told that Planet Ladder represents security. We were promised that the four solid legs of Planet Ladder would support us. We followed the employable sausage route to its logical conclusion, and here we are embracing Planet Ladder.

For many of us, indeed for most of us, citizenship of Planet Ladder means that we have arrived at the place we always expected to be. Apart from having to familiarise ourselves with new surroundings, most of us adapt quite quickly to the employment situation.

The actual process of becoming citizens of Planet Ladder is relatively smooth. After all, we share a set of expectations with our employers about the nature of the employment deal. In exchange for our efforts, Planet Ladder will pay us a regular wage and will manage us within a logical corporate hierarchy. So long as we behave reasonably and perform adequately on Planet Ladder, we can reasonably look forward to steady employment with a steady income and steady prospects.

Once we have taken that first critical step and become used to standing on our particular rung of the ladder, it does not take long for us to set our sights on the next rung. Promotion is a natural goal. Very few people enter the job market harbouring the ambition of remaining at the entry-level job for the rest of their working life. It is normal to want to progress up the ladder, to seek promotion, to be given greater responsibility, and to be paid a higher salary.

And so the process continues. We strive to climb higher and higher on our ladder. For most of us, this is the pattern that we will follow for the rest of our working life.

If you are familiar with *The Peter Principle: Why things always go wrong* (William Morrow & Company, 1969), the brainchild of Laurence Johnston Peter, you will know that this highly entertaining book describes some of the pitfalls of Planet Ladder organisations.

Peter observed that, when new employees in the lower ranks prove to be competent in the task to which they are assigned, they get promoted to a higher rank.

This process of climbing up the hierarchical ladder continues indefinitely, until the employee cannot be promoted any further, thus ending up in a position where he or she is no longer competent. In other words, employees tend to be promoted up to their "level of incompetence".

As a result, Peter argues, most of the higher levels of a bureaucracy are filled by incompetent people, who cannot be got rid of.

Sometimes, when we are the subordinates of these people, our frustration can push us to look for an alternative place of work. And, even if we are still battling to be promoted further up in our organisation, some of us discover that life on Planet Ladder fails to live up to the hype. Despite all the build-up and positive propaganda, some of us are disappointed to discover that we're not enjoying the Planet Ladder experience.

There are several reasons for this initial disappointment. It could be because we don't like the work. Maybe it's because we don't like the people. It might even be that we don't like the pay.

Most of us can take this initial disappointment in our stride. Diamonds might be forever, but ladders are not. If we don't like our ladder, it is quite acceptable to take corrective action. We don't have to remain stuck on one ladder for life. The era of "job for life" is long gone. Indeed, it is rare today to meet anyone who has worked for a single employer all their working life.

Ladder-hopping is perfectly respectable and, in normal economic conditions (when there is no recession), we can nearly always find another ladder that will employ us. And another. And another. Until we get it right.

There are different factors driving our decision to hop off our current ladder and hop on to another ladder.

Sometimes, the decision is voluntary. For example, if we are looking for more rapid advancement than our present employer is prepared to offer, or if we feel like a change.

Sometimes we hop off our ladder because we are poached by another ladder. For example, we can be quite content on our present ladder, with no immediate plans to leave, when out of the blue, another ladder comes along and makes us an offer we can't refuse. If the carrot being dangled in front of us is persuasive enough – the prospect of a bigger salary, bigger social benefits, greater responsibility, or a bigger car – we may well be tempted to hop ladders.

Sometimes our hopping off the ladder is not voluntary, but imposed. The most widespread example is if our employer closes down. Whether we like it or not, our ladder collapses. Another example is when the ladder we're on decides to release us in the name of downsizing. This leaves us with no choice but to find another ladder to hop on to.

Most ladder-hoppers eventually reach a sort of equilibrium. Whether the hopping is driven by dissatisfaction, opportunity or necessity, we hope to eventually settle on a ladder that suits us.

We have focused in this chapter on the process by which we become acclimatised to Planet Ladder. Bob Black in his ***The Abolition of Work*** (Loompanics Unlimited, 1985) could have been describing Planet Ladder when he wrote:

> *People who are regimented all their lives, handed to work from school and bracketed by the family in the beginning and the nursing home at the end, are habituated to hierarchy and psychologically enslaved. Their aptitude for autonomy is so atrophied that their fear of freedom is among their few rationally grounded phobias. Their obedience training at work carries over into the families they start, thus reproducing the system in more ways than one, and into politics, culture, and everything else. Once you drain the vitality from people at work, they'll likely submit to hierarchy and expertise in everything. They're used to it.*

Schools have done a good job conditioning us for Planet Ladder. They take their function as being glorified sausage-processing plants very seriously. They teach us how to pass exams and get our qualifications, and they programme us to reach certain levels of competence in order to fill jobs in the workplace.

Our parents swallow the school line without questioning.

Case Study

During the discussion period in one of my seminars, one of the participants told us of an incident that had happened that very afternoon with her young son.

He was just home from attending his very first day at school. With a mother's natural concern, she asked him how his day had been.

"Fine, Mum, " he replied.

His father entered the room. Pulling himself to his full height, he towered over the wee fellow.

"Son," he said, "Do you realise that today you began a life sentence of hard labour? From today, and for the next 10 years, you're going to be doing hard labour at school. For the following 45 years, you're going to be doing hard labour working for someone else. Not much of a life to look forward to, is it?"

This fatalistic view of the world, as expressed by a young father in 2002, eloquently if negatively summed up what life on Planet Ladder held in store for the young son.

In this chapter, we have described how every element of our society buys into the sausage processing mentality begun in the schools. With our parents so eager to promote the same message, it is easy to see how we are conditioned from early childhood to accept that the reason we go to school is to get a good job on Planet Ladder.

Observers like psychologist Lawrence Kubie may criticise schools and families alike for failing to prepare us adequately for the realities of the adult world, but the fact is that we are surrounded by very powerful stimuli that are constantly pushing us to want to become citizens of Planet Ladder.

Which makes it all the more astonishing that anyone would want to escape.

Yet some of us do. In the next chapter, we will ask why, and at what stage, we start acknowledging that maybe we don't belong on Planet Ladder.

Chapter 6
The Planet Where They Speak Entreprenese

The realisation that we want something different from Planet Ladder can hit us at different times.

There are people around who have always known instinctively that the employment route was not the only option, who knew that society in general and school in particular were not presenting a balanced picture of the world. These people never saw their future as being tied permanently to Planet Ladder.

From early childhood, they have planned to eventually work for themselves. They knew that there was an alternative route to take – the entrepreneurial route, the route where you do your own thing, the route where you become your own boss, the route where you start your own business. These people did not need a roadmap telling them how to leave Planet Ladder. They simply knew the way out.

But for the rest of us, it can be very confusing.

On the one hand we have schools, third level educational institutions and parents telling us that there is no viable alternative to paid employment.

On the other hand, we just have to look around to know that this is simply not so. As we grew older, we cannot fail to see that working for someone else is not the only show in town.

We all grow up coming into contact with people – including our own parents, sometimes – who run their own business. Yet we hear very little about this alien species while we're at school. Self-employment barely registers among the future life choices that are discussed at school.

It is tempting to claim that schools and parents practice mass denial, and that they ignore the fact that not everyone is comfortable in the employment world. They give little priority to encouraging us to seek our own path in life. Their obsession with performance and exam results can blind them to the fact that there are alternatives to Planet Ladder. They ignore the fact that some of us will eventually opt for self-employment.

At what stage in the process do we start feeling trapped by the confines of Planet Ladder? What triggers the realisation that Planet Ladder may not be for us? When do we start looking for other options?

One of the first giveaway signs of feeling trapped is the realisation that it is no longer just this or that particular ladder that we don't like. We notice that we don't like ladders. Any ladders.

Our aversion to ladders is accompanied by several other symptoms. We realise that we no longer like being told what to do. We feel constrained by rules and regulations set by others. We believe that we are doomed to be smarter than any boss (especially if the Peter Principle is correct, and our boss is one level above his or her level of competence.) We realise that, on Planet Ladder, we will never be able to increase our earnings beyond our salaries.

Despite the best efforts of our schools and our parents, some of us conclude that ladder life is not for us. We no longer feel comfortable with ladder life. We start believing that ladder life can actually be bad for our health. To paraphrase the title of a 1960s musical, some of us feel like shouting: "Stop The Ladder, I Want To Get Off".

Getting off one ladder in order to hop on to another is easy. You simply give in your notice. But when we develop a strong antipathy to ladder life, ladder-hopping is no longer a realistic option.

Because when we decide that Planet Ladder is no longer to be our home, when we decide to opt for the entrepreneurial alternative, we reach a moment of truth.

We cross a Rubicon.

For at that moment, we are deciding to change our citizenship. We are preparing ourselves mentally to hand in our Planet Ladder passport.

And where do we go?

To Planet DoingItMyWay.

By exchanging our Planet Ladder passport for a Planet DoingItMyWay passport, we embark on a very fundamental process of transition.

We have to learn to live in a totally different culture. We have to give up the security of Planet Ladder, and learn to stand on our own two feet on Planet DoingItMyWay.

In his best-selling book ***Men are from Mars, Women are from Venus*** (Harper Collins, 1992), John Gray tells us something we all knew instinctively but had rarely put into words – that, in order to understand how men and women interact, we must first acknowledge that they come from two different planets.

Gray claims that the citizens of each planet – the men from Mars and the women from Venus – have a different way of thinking, a different way of acting, and a different way of reacting.

Allan and Barbara Pease take a similar approach in their book ***Why Men Don't Listen and Women Can't Read Maps*** (Pease Training International, 1999). They too spotlight the different ways that men and women think, and the fundamentally different way that men and women relate to the world around them.

The conclusion of both books is similar: by differentiating between the two planets, we can help men obtain better tools for understanding their womenfolk, and we can help women gain a sharper awareness of what will and what won't work with their menfolk.

I mention these two books because I believe we can draw a similar conclusion in the realm of self-employment. Gray and the Peases claim that men and women are from two different planets. I believe that we will gain a better grasp of the family support issue if we regard budding entrepreneurs and their employee families as also coming from two different planets.

To paraphrase Gray, "Employees are from Planet Ladder, the self-employed are from Planet DoingItMyWay".

Just as men and women have different ways of thinking, so employees and the self-employed have different ways of thinking.

When citizens of Planet Ladder opt for citizenship of Planet DoingItMyWay, the newly-naturalised citizens have to learn a completely new way of thinking. They have to learn a new language with its own vocabulary based on its own set of attitudes.

This language is "Entreprenese".

And like any language, Entreprenese consists of a kind of shorthand of ideas which help make communication quicker and more efficient. Entreprenese is a language that incorporates shared entrepreneurial concepts, shared entrepreneurial experiences and shared entrepreneurial perspectives.

If we want to learn Entreprenese, we don't have to enroll in a Berlitz school. Remarkably, the very act of becoming a new citizen of Planet DoingItMyWay helps us pick up Entreprenese almost overnight.

Entreprenese speakers use phrases such as:

- I'm not comfortable working within an organisation.
- I wasn't cut out to bide my time and work my way up the ladder.
- I know I can make a go of it on my own.
- I have fire in the belly.
- I have passion.
- I have vision.
- I have energy.

- I am motivated.
- I see potential where others see disaster.
- I see solutions where others think it can't be done.
- I have the chutzpah to believe I can make it on my own.
- I have the chutzpah to embark on a new venture with no guarantee that it will succeed.
- I have the chutzpah to compete with established companies in my field.
- I have a strong need to be independent.
- I am defined by my need for freedom.
- I don't like being told what to do.
- I want to be a participant, not an observer.
- I don't accept that just because something hasn't been done before, I shouldn't try it.
- I have belief in myself and in what I am trying to create.
- I prefer to rely on myself than on anyone else.
- I don't waste time wondering whether I did the right thing.
- I don't like sitting around waiting for things to happen.
- I have a long-term perspective.
- I allow my imagination to take me on fascinating journeys.
- I am willing to bend the rules, to be different.
- I believe in listening to my instincts.
- I am prepared to live with a degree of uncertainty.
- I thrive in an unstructured environment.
- I am not devastated by failure.
- I am prepared to work round the clock to get something done.
- I am prepared to forgo a social life while I'm getting my business up and running.

For a glimpse of what happens when we wake up with these new language skills, let's revisit Daddy Bear's entrepreneurial announcement scene.

When Daddy Bear comes bouncing home to share his good news with Mummy Bear, he is speaking Entreprenese.

And that's where the problems begin.

There is an inevitable clash of expectations. When Daddy Bear announces his intention to start a new business, he is speaking a new language. He has swapped citizenship, he has a new passport.

But what about Mummy Bear? She doesn't understand this new language. She happily clings to her familiar Planet Ladder attitudes. For her, Entreprenese sounds as strange as Chinese.

So when Daddy Bear excitedly jabbers away in Entreprenese about his plans to start his own business, he is met by a wall of incomprehension.

It is not difficult to guess what's going through Mummy Bear's mind:

*Here he is, the man I love – and he sounds like he's **ON** something. He's talking a language I don't understand. I'm scared. I feel threatened. My man has been bitten by a strange bug. He used to be normal, now he's acting weird.*

Mummy Bear has difficulty understanding Entreprenese because she is a citizen of Planet Ladder, a planet that represents safety and security.

This is the world she knows and understands. She is comfortable with other Planet Ladder citizens. And, until this morning, she thought that her husband was also a Planet Ladder citizen.

There is only one bit of information that Mummy Bear is able to pick up from Daddy Bear's strange-sounding Entreprenese words.

He intends to leave Planet Ladder.

So Mummy Bear does the only reasonable thing she knows under the circumstances.

She panics.

When she reacts to Daddy Bear's entrepreneurial announcement by questioning his mental health ("You're mad"; "You're out of your mind"; "You're having a nervous breakdown"), she is merely reflecting traditional Planet Ladder concerns.

When she expresses outrage ("How dare you!"; "How can you be so irresponsible"), she is merely reflecting normal Planet Ladder reactions.

When she puts Daddy Bear down ("Get real"; "You'll never make it"; "You don't have a chance of succeeding"), she is merely reflecting her Planet Ladder upbringing.

When she issues threats or ultimatums ("Over my dead body"; "Read my lips – No, you're not"), she is merely succumbing to the conditioning she has received throughout her Planet Ladder life.

Daddy Bear dreams of being off the ladder. Mummy Bear thinks he's off his rocker.

Mummy Bear's problems are not confined just to language. We're talking here about a fundamentally different way of thinking. Citizens of Planet Ladder and Planet DoingItMyWay have different behaviour and thought patterns.

Take attitudes to time, for example. During the course of a working day, Planet Ladder citizens probably look at their wrist watches dozens of times. What do they see? Twelve equidistant numbers on the clock face?

No.

They see the time in relation to the 9-to-5 spectrum. In other words, they see the time in terms of the distance between arriving at work at the start of the day, and leaving work at the end of the day.

For example, if it's 10.30, Planet Ladder citizens can't help but make the mental note that it's 30 minutes to their coffee break.

If it's 12.30, they know it'll soon be lunchtime.

If it's 4.30, they are already on a countdown to the time they can go home.

If it's after 6, they wonder why they're not home yet – or they're busy calculating their overtime pay.

This obsessive focus on "how long since..." or "how long before..." does not mean that Planet Ladder citizens are bad people or disloyal employees. When you spend your day in someone else's employ, your day will be inevitably be centred around the amount of time you spend at your workplace.

Now let's look at the clock face of Entreprenese speakers. They too do not see 12 equidistant numbers. That's because most entrepreneurs will tell you that they have to squeeze more than 24 hours into a day.

When entrepreneurs look at their watches, it's always the *wrong* time! There is always something else that needs urgent attention. There is always something else that should have been completed by now.

As veteran humourist Sam Ewing put it: "It's not the hours you put in your work that counts, it's the work you put in the hours".

The difference between the two planets is that while Planet Ladder citizens make their schedules fit the clock, Planet DoingItMyWay citizens make the clock fit their schedules.

Citizens of Planet Ladder take the smallest job, and try to expand it to take up as much time as possible (without being reprimanded for slacking). Citizens of Planet DoingItMyWay take the largest job, and try to squeeze it into the smallest time frame possible (without compromising on quality), because there is always more to do. The sooner one task is completed, the sooner the next task can be tackled.

In his thought-provoking book **Rich Dad, Poor Dad** (Warner Books, 1997), Robert T Kiyosaki described two fundamentally different attitudes to life. He could well have been describing the differences between Planet Ladder and Planet DoingItMyWay.

POOR DAD (Planet Ladder)	RICH DAD (Planet DoingItMyWay)
Tells his children to study hard so they can find a good company to work for.	Tell his children to study hard so they can find a good company to buy.
Tells his children the reason he's not rich is because he has kids.	Tells his children the reason he must be rich is because he has kids.
Forbids the subject of money to be discussed over a meal.	Encourages talking about money and business at the dinner table.
Believes that the company should take care of you and your needs.	Believes in total financial self-reliance.
Is always concerned about pay rises, retirement plans, medical benefits, sick leave, vacation days and other perks.	Stresses the need to be financially competent.
The idea of job protection for life and job benefits often seems more important than the job.	Speaks out against entitlement mentality.
Teaches his child to write an impressive CV so he/she can find a good job.	Teaches his child to write an impressive business plan so he/she can create jobs.

The citizens of Planet Ladder and Planet DoingItMyWay are separated by a language barrier.

The Mummy Bears who live on Planet Ladder cannot understand Entreprenese, the adopted language of the Daddy Bears who have moved to Planet DoingItMyWay – and the Daddy Bears are frustrated at the inability of Mummy Bears to learn Entreprenese.

In these circumstances, how can we expect families to jump for joy when faced with the trauma of a family member who seems to have gone off the rails?

Does this prevent most budding entrepreneurs from going ahead with their entrepreneurial plans anyway?

No.

But, even if the negative reactions from family don't leave scars, many entrepreneurs assume that once they survive the initial hurdles, the family might get used to the idea in time.

Unfortunately, this too is wishful thinking.

As we will see in the next chapter, Entreprenese speakers who suffer from the lack of universal on-tap emotional support from their family when they open their business, can have an even tougher time when they take the plunge and enter the start-up phase.

Chapter 7
Lonely at the Top

Notwithstanding actor Sir Anthony Hopkins' comment that anyone who says it's lonely at the top needs either a good psychiatrist or a kick up the arse, the sense of loneliness is the one thing shared by almost anyone who makes the leap to become their own boss.

The famous philosopher Friedrich Nietzsche eloquently described this feeling:

The individual has always had to struggle to keep from being overwhelmed by the tribe. If you try it, you will be lonely often, and sometimes frightened. But no price is too high to pay for the privilege of owning yourself.

The loneliness felt by so many entrepreneurs is a theme that never fails to be articulated by participants in my seminars.

Whether we are talking about people who have just started out, or those who have been in business for years, the feedback is almost universally consistent.

Most entrepreneurs claim that loneliness is the number one problem they encounter.

The loneliness of the entrepreneur is all the more problematic because it is so unexpected. The sense of isolation felt by people who run their own business comes as a shock to them. No one had warned them about it, and they were not mentally prepared for it.

The sense of loneliness has been succinctly described in this illuminating passage by Timothy F. McCarthy, the CEO of Sales Building Systems, Ohio:

> *The toughest challenge is overcoming loneliness. When I opened my business after being fired as the head of marketing for a large restaurant chain, I was prepared for aspects of business I wasn't used to, like having to sell all the time. And I was prepared for the fear of doing it on my own. But I wasn't prepared for the loneliness, especially in the first year. I hadn't realised how much support you get, in terms of both systems and people, from a regular-size company. But when you're on your own, the value of that support is obvious: having a real person at a nearby desk to bitch with, or having a legal department and a human resources department. Now that I've succeeded, I help others start businesses, and when I warn them how lonely it is, they get this look of disbelief. 'Just wait until that first time you find you've got no one else to count on, and you'll see', I tell them.*

When we first get the idea of becoming our own boss, it can all be very intoxicating. We tell ourselves that here is our opportunity to throw off the shackles we associate with corporate life. We look forward to Planet DoingItMyWay, to being part of a world where there are no bosses telling us what to do. We welcome the opportunity to do things our own way. We welcome the sense of empowerment that starting our own business brings. We rejoice that we will no longer have to put up with other people's stupidities.

In the run-up period prior to actually opening our new venture, we're kept very busy. There are a million and one things that need to be done. The countdown to the launch date tends to consume all our attention. There's far too much going on to feel lonely. If our family are on board, great. If they're not, too bad.

Then the big day comes – and passes. The opening day can often turn into an anti-climax. We've opened our doors, our business is officially up and running, and we're suddenly on our own.

And it's lonely.

However much we have mentally prepared ourselves to have to do everything on our own, however much we believe that we understand the meaning of "the buck stops here", we often haven't given this too much thought.

Confucius put it very eloquently when he said, "Top of mountain great place. But very lonely".

Theologian and philosopher Paul Johannes Tillich said that the English language offers us the two sides of being alone: the word **loneliness** expresses the **pain** of being alone; the word **solitude** expresses the **glory** of being alone.

There is little doubt that it is loneliness that is felt by entrepreneurs.

Why does the sense of isolation and loneliness hit us like this?

Why is it that so many people who run their own business suddenly find that they have no one to turn to?

Why do we suffer from what I describe in *Fire in the Belly* as "the loneliness of the long-distance entrepreneur?"

In the context of the myth of the universality of family support, the feeling of loneliness is part of the transition process from employee to self-employed, from citizen of Planet Ladder to citizen of Planet DoingItMyWay.

That's because before, during and after we make this transition, we often forget that the price we pay is that our normal supports desert us.

The extent to which we have to leave behind our familiar support systems when we start our own business is illustrated by the following two case studies.

Case Study

Cassie worked as a telephonist on the switchboard of a busy office. She not only handled incoming calls from the general public, but also helped route calls among the various departments.

One morning, she received a call from Darren, the manager of one of the departments. He was looking for Mandy, the CEO. Cassie tried to trace Mandy, and was informed by Mandy's office manager that she was tied up in a meeting.

When Darren continued to insist that Cassie get him through to Mandy, Cassie politely informed him that she could do no more. At this point, Darren became verbally abusive.

Cassie was very upset by this incident. At the first opportunity, she complained about Darren's rudeness to her direct supervisor. She made an official complaint through the appropriate grievance mechanism. During the lunch break, she shared this unpleasant incident with her work colleagues. They were suitably shocked, and encouraged Cassie to follow through on her complaint.

When Cassie got home at the end of the working day, she was able to let off steam even further. She knew she could expect the full sympathy of everyone in the family. She was not disappointed. Darren's name became dirt in the Cassie household. And eventually, Darren was forced to apologise to her at work as well.

As a citizen of Planet Ladder, Cassie took it for granted that she could and would receive support from others. When she encountered a problem, she knew she could always turn to two trusted sources for moral support. She knew that she could turn to her colleagues at work, and to her family at home.

Now let's see what happens when we forsake Planet Ladder for other pastures.

Case Study

Despite a highly skeptical attitude from her family and friends, Melanie left her job as a dispatcher with a national courier company in order to set up her own courier business.

Her big breakthrough came when she attended a film festival in Palm Springs. There, she met a movie executive whose company was spending over $10,000 a month working with half a dozen courier services to send press kits, scripts and promotional materials all over Los Angeles. Melanie pitched a proposal that would cut their monthly bill by 40%. The company accepted her bid, and Melanie had her first customer.

At first, things were great. Other work followed from other Hollywood movie companies, and Melanie was sure that she would soon start seeing a profit.

One morning, disaster struck. Her bank phoned to tell her that the cheque she had lodged from her first Hollywood client had bounced.

Instinctively, a very upset Melanie turned to her usual supports, looking for a sympathetic ear. She was in for a rude awakening.

She tried to meet up with her former work colleagues in order to share her problem with them. As she started relating her woes, she noticed that her colleagues' eyes were glazing over. They didn't understand the workings of Planet DoingItMyWay, and they were not interested in its problems. They also did not understand why Melanie had left them to start her own business in the first place. It was clear that Melanie could expect no great understanding and support from that quarter.

> When Melanie turned to her second natural source of support – her family – it was even worse. They were still reeling from her decision to leave the security of Planet Ladder to start her own business. They still believed that Melanie must have a screw loose. Informing her family that a cheque had bounced only reinforced their prejudices.

By moving from Planet Ladder to Planet DoingItMyWay, Melanie forfeited her right to automatic knee-jerk support from her family and her work colleagues.

The very people she felt she could turn to proved to be the least likely to be understanding when she tried to share her problem with them.

On Planet Ladder, we are used to being part of a team.

On a bad day, we always have a colleague's shoulder to cry on.

On a good day, there is always someone around to congratulate us.

We have colleagues with whom to share things with. We are used to seeking – and receiving – validation from others. And when we get home, we can draw on further sympathy.

But this changes dramatically when we move to Planet DoingItMyWay. The reason that so many people who start their own business feel lonely is that suddenly they can no longer call upon their normal sources of emotional support.

The very time that entrepreneurs need their family most is the time that they feel let down by family. Just when entrepreneurs need emotional bolstering, they feel that their family can't or won't help them.

Once again, we seem to be stumbling over the myth of on-tap family support and the unrealistic expectations that this creates.

The new citizens of Planet DoingItMyWay face a double whammy.

When they first announce that they wish to embark on their entrepreneurial adventure, they do not receive emotional support from their families.

When their new business is up and running, this negativity often persists. Cut off from their former sources of support, they feel lonely.

How do we get over this? What can we do to compensate for the loneliness of the long distance entrepreneur?

In the next chapter, we will look at some coping strategies, and some alternative sources of support.

Chapter 8
Coping Strategies for Entrepreneurs

In the face of the inability of our families to deliver on-tap emotional support as we set out to create and grow our new business, we need to develop a suite of coping strategies to combat the alienation and negativity that we experience.

If we are not getting the positive feedback we need from home, where can we turn for emotional support?

Source 1: Ourselves

An obvious source of support is to look to our own strengths.

There is no doubt that it helps to be able to draw on our own resources.

It helps to be confident, to have courage, and to have faith in ourselves.

It is also useful to learn to live with the negative opinions of others is an effective way of fighting self-doubt.

It is useful to be able to plug into our reserves of self-esteem, especially when faced with a constant barrage of criticism from people who question our very sanity.

> *Whatever you do, you need courage. Whatever course you decide upon, there is always someone to tell you that you are wrong. There are always difficulties arising which tempt you to believe that your critics are right. To map out a course of action and follow it to the end, requires some of the same courage which a soldier needs. (Ralph Waldo Emerson, American writer, philosopher, poet and essayist)*

Our survival on Planet DoingItMyWay depends on our ability to fight against self-doubt, to avoid the temptation of secretly suspecting that others may be right when they tell us that we'll never succeed. This is where a healthy dose of self-esteem and self-belief can come in very useful.

The self-esteem movement has come in for some bad press in recent times. There seems to be a new fashion in articles and books to debunk self-esteem as an empty concept that cannot be quantified and is therefore meaningless.

This is not the place to get side-tracked into a debate on this issue.

I would just say that my experience of the "Start Your Own Business" field has shown that self-esteem, self-belief and self-confidence can be very useful counterweights in overcoming human and financial obstacles.

It is only natural to want approval from others. But ultimately we must learn to be able to survive without that approval. The more we legitimise our own feelings and actions, the more we can manage without such approval.

Source 2: Entrepreneurs in the Family

There is another source of support that we should not totally discount.

Even if most members of the family react negatively to our entrepreneurial plans, it does not mean that *every* member of our extended family is necessarily a citizen of Planet Ladder. It can be instructive to conduct a little family research. Maybe there is a cousin, an uncle, an aunt somewhere who has started a business. Maybe there is someone in the family who is married to, or living with, a citizen of Planet DoingItMyWay.

It is worth actively seeking out such people.

Ask them how they coped with family criticism. You may get some valuable tips on how to handle the volatile issue of entrepreneurial ventures in this particular family. Who knows, these people may well have encountered identical reactions from the very people who were so quick to share their negative opinions with you.

Source 3: Role Models

The Ernst & Young/London School of Economics report mentioned earlier points to another source of support: inspiring public figures.

Role models like Alex Ferguson (Manchester United), Richard Branson (Virgin) and Bill Gates (Microsoft) are frequently mentioned. Many people avidly read biographies of famous entrepreneurs in order to seek inspiration.

CASE STUDY

> While conducting research for a book I am writing on Chutzpah, that evocative word that is a combination of cheek, nerve, audacity, guts, gall, outrageousness, effrontery, bottle, gumption, sauciness, boldness and balls, I came across the story of inventor, James Dyson.
>
> While renovating his country house, he noticed that the new bag in his Junior Hoover kept clogging, and had very little suction.
>
> "There's got to be a better way", he said to himself. "I'm going to invent the first bagless vacuum cleaner".
>
> His search turned into an obsession. Over the next four years, Dyson built no fewer than 5,127 prototypes until he finally came up with his revolutionary Dual Cyclone vacuum cleaner.

I used this example in a seminar for recent start-up business owner/managers on the dogged single-mindedness you need when you run your own business.

Before I got to the punch-line, one of the participants piped up: "5,127 prototypes!".

Dyson's example had so impressed the young man that he knew every detail of Dyson's career by heart. Dyson was a constant source of inspiration to this new entrepreneur as he struggled to conquer his loneliness.

Source 4: Phone-a-Friend

But there is still one under-explored and under-utilised source of support that never fails us.

Earlier, we charted the problems that arise when we try and engage in conversation with someone who does not speak Entreprenese. We identified that one of the core reasons why families can't give emotional support is that they do not understand our language.

So, instead of expending so much energy getting upset with all those who cannot help us, why not turn to those who can?

Why not seek out others who are guaranteed to speak our language?

Why not seek out other entrepreneurs who have walked the entrepreneurial walk, who have survived the traumas of starting up on their own, and with whom you can converse in Entreprenese?

According to the Ernst & Young/London School of Economics report, 20% of entrepreneurs do in fact fall back on friends to help launch their business, filling the gap left by families.

Case Study

When Julia turned up at one of my seminars, she had been a self-employed ceramic artist for over two years. She told us that her business was thriving, she had a full order-book, and everything was fine - except that she was having difficulty coping with the loneliness.

Julia was acutely aware that her support system had disappeared from under her feet. Her family had never believed that she should go out on her own at such an early age, and they found it hard to relate to this combination of gifted artist and wily businesswoman.

Desperate for some positive reinforcement, Julia had hit upon a solution.

"Every couple of months, I phone a friend of mine in Paris who runs her own art gallery. All I need to hear are three magic words: 'Julia, you're wonderful'.

"It's like getting a regular fix of emotional support", Julia told us. "It's not enough for me to know that I'm good at my work and that my business is successful. I need to be told that I'm OK, that I'm doing the right thing. I can't get this feedback from my family or friends. So I get it from someone who speaks my language, who knows what it's like to be alone. And it works. Being told that I'm wonderful by a fellow entrepreneur keeps me going for the next few weeks".

We can all take a leaf out of Julia's book and phone a friend. With so many others who have gone through the same process, there is no need to be alone out there. Other entrepreneurs will be happy to listen and to share, because they will almost certainly have experienced the same sense of loneliness themselves.

I consider myself lucky, because I have found two loyal entrepreneurial friends who fit the phone-a-friend description.

Alan runs a PR company in Scotland, and I know that I can call him at any time, and share with him stuff that I know he can identify with. I can complain about the workflow, vent my anger at clients who abuse my goodwill, or curse the postal system for delivering the cheques late, and the banking system for charging me so much.

My other phone-a-friend is Gráinne, who runs her own marketing consultancy company in Ireland. Her familiarity with the Irish business scene, and her willingness to share this with me, means that I call her instinctively if I want to mull over an idea.

And this is fully reciprocated. They know that I will always make time to hear them out if they want to let off steam or share a triumph.

Your phone-a-friend is a perspective-providing peer who acts as a personal guide and mentor. Your phone-a-friend is the first person you phone when faced with a problem that cannot be fixed by professional experts. Your phone-a-friend must share your passionate belief in the centrality of being your own boss in your life. Your phone-a-friend will give you frank, realistic, appropriate and personal feedback. Your phone-a-friend will help you avoid pitfalls and mistakes that they made in their own business. Your phone-a-friend will know enough about you to give you advice that combines the professional and the personal.

Source 5: Mutual Support Groups

Entrepreneurs often create informal mutual support groups, even if they do not necessarily define them as such.

If we want to counter the loneliness and sense of isolation that is the entrepreneur's lot, we should actively seek out others in the same boat.

The benefits we gain from this more than make up for the disappointment of not getting the support we crave from our family.

CASE STUDY

Gillian ran her own office machines business in a small town in rural Ireland. Over the years, she and a few other business owners in the town, both men and women, had got into the habit of meeting up at the end of the working week late on a Friday afternoon.

Gillian and her colleagues always went to the same pub and sat around the same table. They would chat about their week. None of the group were direct competitors and, although the purpose of the weekly get-together was not specifically to network, some of them had started doing business with each other.

One week, as the group were swapping stories around the table, they were joined by Michael, a newcomer to town who ran a website design company. One of the group knew Michael, and invited him to join them. He was quickly absorbed into the flow of conversation, and it was clear that he had been accepted into the group. To avoid any misunderstanding, Michael was specifically invited to join the informal Friday afternoon get-together.

The next week, the local bank manager Philip happened to be in the same pub. Out of politeness, and because most of the group knew him, Philip was invited to join the crowd around the table. Within minutes, the conversation dried up. The buzz that marked the weekly get-together fizzled out. Gillian and her friends were embarrassed, and could not put their finger on what had happened.

It was only when Gillian attended a seminar where we discussed the Phone a Friend idea that she realised what had transpired. As she told us:

"Now I see the dynamics in a new light. We are a bunch of self-employed entrepreneurs who have naturally gravitated to each other out of a need to talk Entreprenese. We deliberately sought out other citizens of Planet DoingItMyWay who understand the language. Without spelling it out, we had created an informal mutual support group where we all felt entirely comfortable. So it's no wonder that, when a Ladder Planet citizen joined the chat, we dried up. We were all too aware that Philip does not speak Entreprenese. Our comfort zone was immediately affected, and we ran out of things to say."

CHAPTER 9
BRIDGING THE COMMUNICATION GAP

We have seen that the citizens of Planet Ladder and Planet DoingItMyWay are separated by a language barrier. The Mummy Bears on Planet Ladder cannot understand Entreprenese, the adopted language of the Daddy Bears on Planet DoingItMyWay – and the Daddy Bears are frustrated at Mummy Bear's inability to learn Entreprenese.

Clearly, any meaningful dialogue between the people wanting to start their own business and their families must also involve an acknowledgement of this language barrier, of this communication gap.

This makes it all the more urgent for anyone with an entrepreneurial bee in their bonnet to adopt strategies to "handle" their families better, to communicate their hopes and aspirations in a more effective way.

Budding entrepreneurs must acknowledge the existence of two different mindsets. This will help them appreciate the need for a more subtle approach when they make their entrepreneurial announcement.

They need to employ better communication skills when they break the entrepreneurial news to their family.

They need a more compassionate understanding of how their venture will affect their home life and family.

Entrepreneurs can avail of several basic skills, techniques and strategies to help bridge this communication gap:

- Negotiation
- Listening
- Accommodation, not victory
- Not getting personal
- Choosing the right place and the right time
- Trade-off.

Negotiation

Negotiation is a highly sophisticated form of communication. Try treating the entrepreneurial announcement as an exercise in negotiation. Don't be alarmed by the idea that you need to negotiate with your family.

Negotiation is a useful tool in conflict situations, where what we want is not necessarily what someone else wants.

If we want the outcome to be a solution that we can both live with, rather than a protracted fight, then negotiation is what we should turn to.

Most of us use negotiation skills on a daily basis, probably more often than we realise.

At work, at home and at recreation, we are constantly involved in potential conflict situations that can be resolved through negotiation. There are lots of situations where choosing negotiation over confrontation leaves both sides with their self-respect intact – **and** gets the job done. For example, every time we try to convince a child or an employee to complete a chore they don't really want to do, negotiation mode is often more successful than confrontation mode.

As we have seen, our entrepreneurial announcement has the potential to create conflict. By acknowledging this in advance, we can choose to try negotiating techniques instead.

By accepting that we are not going to receive the enthusiastic response we might have wished for in an ideal world, we will be better prepared mentally to engage in a dialogue with our family.

The whole way we frame our announcement can be different.

If we start by acknowledging in advance that our family may not see things like us, we have a healthy basis for negotiation. By looking beyond our business plans and thinking in terms of creating a workable family strategy, we can look forward to achieving a negotiated outcome that we can all live with.

Listening

When we plan in our minds how we are going to communicate our entrepreneurial aspirations to family members, we know precisely what we want to achieve – and we also have a certain level of expectation regarding the reaction we want to hear.

But unless we learn to see beyond our own inner dialogue, we are dooming ourselves to an encounter full of recriminations. That is why listening is such an essential ingredient in negotiating.

If we are not also prepared to listen, we will lose communication.

When we negotiate, we need to turn off our inner voice and concentrate on listening. As soon as our entrepreneurial announcement starts sounding like preaching, real dialogue will go out the window.

We are going to have to use all our listening skills if we want to catch important nonverbal messages, facial expressions and voice inflections.

By genuinely listening to the concerns and fears that our family is expressing, we are in a better position to find a mutually satisfactory resolution.

Above all, by listening, we can avoid getting into a slanging match.

It is impossible to create an atmosphere of constructive dialogue when we are all too busy trying to insist that our truth is the only truth.

It is useful to remember that Entreprenese is a foreign language for our family.

If a cousin came to visit us from a country where English is not the first language, we would take extra care in communicating with them. We would take care to express ourselves more clearly. We would check every couple of minutes that our cousin understood what we were saying.

It is the same with the entrepreneurial announcement.

We must listen intently to make sure that we are making ourselves understood. And we must listen intently to the reactions without feeling unsupported, misunderstood and under-appreciated.

By becoming better listeners, we can lower the stress level of the person we're talking to. When the subject matter is emotionally charged, as it is when we are trying to communicate our desire to start our own business, we have a better chance of communicating if we listen in a reassuring, caring and understanding manner.

Another thing to pay attention to is when we hear ourselves doing most of the talking. After we bring up the subject and explain our plans, at a certain point we should stop and remember to listen. We should encourage our partner to ask questions or comment, and to address their concerns rather than try and prove that we are right. We should also try not to interrupt. Remaining in listening mode is our best policy.

Accommodation, not victory

We will achieve better and more fruitful communication if we remember that we are not seeking an outcome with only one winner. By focussing on the ultimate outcome, we can avoid the temptation to "win the argument".

We must always bear in mind that the objective of negotiation is to reach an accommodation, not to score a victory. The whole point of honest negotiations is to reach an outcome where everyone wins.

After all, we have a strong interest in a continuing relationship with the person we are negotiating with – in this case, our family.

Clearly, when we wish to announce impending changes of great significance, it won't help our cause if we go about it like the proverbial bull in a china shop.

The last thing we want is for the other person to feel that he or she has been browbeaten or defeated. Our entrepreneurial announcement should be the opening stage of our dialogue, not a *fait accompli*.

The cost of failure or unwillingness to reach some sort of accommodation is further strife and tension. It would be a hollow victory indeed if we won our battle but lost our family in the process.

There is an alternative, and that is a commitment to an outcome that has been negotiated, not forced. Our goal is a win-win situation where both sides feel they have emerged with something. We are not seeking an outcome where one side feels they have lost, or an outcome where both sides feel that they have lost.

And even if we cannot always achieve the accommodation we seek, it is better to agree to differ than to end the discussion with one of the parties walking away in a huff.

Not getting personal

It is very tempting in a highly-charged atmosphere to get personal.

By separating people from the problem, our negotiations can proceed in a more constructive atmosphere. That is why we should steer the discussion away from personalities, and concentrate on addressing the issue at hand. Getting personal can only lead to even more entrenched positions. We have to learn to let the other person blow off steam without taking it personally.

All negotiations involve both a rational decision-making process and an emotional process.

Rational arguments are not enough, and can even make matters worse if we ignore the emotional element. There is no point trying to argue with another person's feelings, and we should learn to acknowledge another's right to be emotionally upset. The best thing we can do is try and understand where they are coming from.

We need to remember that they have a right to think differently from us.

We must be especially careful to monitor our reactions when the other person becomes visibly upset by what we are saying. We should avoid adding fuel to the fire with comments like: "You always only see problems", "You never listen to what I'm saying", or "I can't talk to you when you're so upset".

And if we are on the receiving end of comments like "You always spring surprises on me at the wrong moment", it is *our* responsibility to avoid getting personal.

Because let's not forget which is the chicken and which is the egg. If we are the one to announce our entrepreneurial intentions, it is we who are disturbing the momentum. We are in control. We should remember this if the atmosphere heats up. It is our responsibility to cool things down, to diffuse the personal bit.

Every conflict situation contains the potential for magnifying perceived differences and minimising similarities.

One of the negative results of personalising a conflict is that we are in danger of rocking the foundations of harmony and commonality of purpose that we have worked so hard to build and which underpin healthy family life.

We must remember, and we must gently remind our negotiating partner, that our decision to leave Planet Ladder is not a personal statement designed to undermine the other person. We have not changed our commitment to sharing with our family a desire for a secure financial future. Even if we are now choosing the entrepreneurial route, we still share with our family a common commitment to our future.

If we are interested in achieving real dialogue, the trick is to try and stick to the issues, without getting side-tracked, and without getting personal.

Our success in not getting hooked into emotional reactions, and in avoiding falling into a recrimination cycle, will ultimately help us negotiate more effectively.

Choosing the right place and the right time

We have to give careful thought to the venue for the discussion. And since we are the ones who want to share our entrepreneurial dreams with our family, we are the ones who have to create the right environment for our entrepreneurial announcement. Responsibility for setting the tone of the discussion with family members lies squarely with us, the ones who are initiating the discussion.

It is worth asking ourselves what is the most suitable physical space for making our entrepreneurial announcement and for the subsequent negotiations. We have to choose a space where we are both comfortable. We should avoid a space where either of us might feel uncomfortable, or where one of us might feel at a disadvantage.

In order to help diffuse tension, it is worth considering a neutral venue where we both can talk without feeling intimidated. For example, if we suspect that discussing this issue at home could give either of us an unfair strategic advantage, then maybe we should look elsewhere.

Our goal is to find a venue where honest dialogue can take place. We need to find a venue that is appropriate for a discussion. A cosy restaurant may be more suitable as a venue for serious discussion than a crowded and noisy bar.

In addition to choosing the right place, we also have to look for the right time – and the right timing. We should choose a time of day when both of us are fit for a fruitful discussion, and we should avoid times when we are tired. No one ever performs well when they are tired.

Timing is also important. A discussion about our entrepreneurial plans should not be rushed. We should leave ourselves adequate time to engage in a meaningful dialogue. For example, trying to squeeze our entrepreneurial announcement into a one-minute window between the end of the meal and getting the kids off to bed is asking for trouble.

It all comes back to remembering whose initiative this is. Ours.

We want to discuss our entrepreneurial future, so we must set the scene, we must judge if the timing is right, and we must allow enough time to give the subject a proper airing.

Trade-off

If we want to communicate our hopes and aspirations in a more effective way, we need to achieve maximum benefit from negotiation mode.

All the skills, techniques and strategies outlined above are geared to achieve an understanding between us and our families. And to ensure that our negotiations achieve a positive result, we must be prepared from the outset for an outcome that involves some kind of trade-off.

This does not mean giving up on our ultimate goal of starting our own business.

But it does mean seeking a way of making our entrepreneurial announcement more acceptable. We have to ask ourselves how we can sweeten the blow, what **we** can do to help make our plans more palatable for our family.

Although we should never enter a negotiating situation expecting miracles, they do sometimes happen. The reaction from our partner, even a Planet Ladder partner, can be surprisingly positive – in which case we should say a little prayer of thanks.

But it is more likely that our announcement will not be received with an overdose of enthusiasm. We have to remember that our goal is to avoid confrontation and conflict. It is therefore our responsibility to think through in advance what sort of trade-off we might try and negotiate.

Trade-off means making concessions. What can we offer in exchange for greater emotional support from our family?

Maybe this is the right time to reconsider our previous resistance to something that our partner really wants. Maybe a softening of our attitude to something they want to do will achieve the trade-off we seek. Maybe we can use this opportunity to offer some compromise in exchange for more understanding from our partner about our entrepreneurial plans.

They say that peace treaties are only negotiated with enemies, not with friendly nations. While Planet Ladder and Planet DoingItMyWay are not enemies, they can have widely different agendas. That is why negotiation may be the best form of communication.

And the object of negotiations is not to win.

We enter negotiations with our Planet Ladder family in order to reach a working agreement, a trade-off that leaves both parties with a road map on how to proceed.

Chapter 10
Coping Strategies for Families

In the preceding chapters, we explored the failure of families to deliver emotional support from the perspective of the entrepreneur. We identified a significant gap between the support we would love to have, and the lack of support we often experience. We tried to warn people who are thinking of starting their own business that they cannot automatically expect the level of support they believe is their due. We explored various ways in which entrepreneurs could maybe adopt a more moderate approach when delivering their entrepreneurial announcement.

In other words, we placed the onus of responsibility squarely on the entrepreneur. We urged the citizens of Planet DoingItMyWay to make allowances for the fact that citizens of Planet Ladder do not speak Entreprenese.

But we also need to explore the issue from the opposite perspective. After all, spouses and significant others feel isolated and lonely too.

So instead of only counselling budding entrepreneurs on how to handle the lack of family support, let's focus on the entrepreneurs' long-suffering Planet Ladder families.

We said earlier that citizens of Planet Ladder find it very difficult to master Entreprenese. In fact, they don't really understand the need to learn a new language in the first place.

They find it strange that anyone would want to leave the comfort zone provided by Planet Ladder. They do not understand the causal connection between complaining about one's job and starting one's own business.

From their perspective, complaining about your place of employment is normal. Starting your own business is not normal.

After all, doesn't everyone complain about their work? As American publisher and businessman Malcolm Stevenson Forbes put it:

If you have a job without aggravation, you don't have a job.

So what's the big deal? What has complaining about your job got to do with wanting to leave Planet Ladder? Why not complain and stay put, like normal people?

Complaining comes with the Planet ladder territory. Everyone complains about their boss. Everyone complains about their pay. Everyone complains about their work colleagues. Everyone complains that work is too boring, too repetitive, too complex. Everyone complains about work conditions.

But disillusionment runs deeper than complaining. When we feel disillusioned, we feel that there's something wrong with the whole system. We feel that no matter how hard we work, no matter how diligent we are, no matter how well we play the game, we cannot win. Deep down, we become turned off by the whole employment experience. Disillusionment makes us rebel against – and ultimately reject – a system where the few direct the work of the many, and where rules and regulations reduce rather than enhance initiative and creativity.

That's why Planet Ladder citizens who move from complaining to disillusionment are more likely to look for options outside the world of employment, outside of Planet Ladder. They are more likely to convert the negative energy of their disillusionment into positive thinking about better alternatives such as starting a business.

Case Study

Ann and Julian worked together in the probation service. Neither of them was happy with their work.

Ann was a complainer. She complained about her boss. She complained about her pay. She complained about her work colleagues. She complained about her work: Too boring, too repetitive. She complained about her work conditions: the central heating, the coffee, the parking arrangements, and a host of other issues.

Julian was disillusioned. He felt that there was something wrong with the whole system. He felt that no matter how hard he worked, no matter how diligent he was, no matter how well he played the game, deep down Ladder life was just not for him.

Like many people who perpetually complain, Ann expended a great deal of negative energy.

"Nothing is right. Life is a pain. There's nothing to be done."

She stayed in her job until she retired, complaining to the bitter end.

Julian's disillusionment contained the seed of positive energy.

"There must be a better way. Life is for living. I have to find a different way of doing things".

Those of us who make the journey from complaining to disillusionment, and from disillusionment to seeking the entrepreneurial route, find this a natural journey.

Our families do not see it like that at all. What they see is that the new citizen of Planet DoingItMyWay is jumping ship and deserting them.

Planet Ladder families ask:

- How can we be expected to deliver support to our loved ones when we feel so threatened by their plans?
- How can anyone expect Planet Ladder families to adopt Planet DoingItMyWay attitudes?
- How are we expected to master Entreprenese?

In this chapter, we will suggest some coping strategies for the families of budding entrepreneurs.

The first thing we can do is to reassure families.

Yes, there are significant differences between Planet Ladder and Planet DoingItMyWay. But that does not mean that the latter is superior to the former. It just means that we can all exercise our free choice as to which planet we wish to live on. We must always remember that the citizens of both planets have an equally valuable contribution to make to society.

I like the way Martin Luther King Jr. described this:

If a man is called to be a streetsweeper, he should sweep streets even as Michelangelo painted, or Beethoven played music, or Shakespeare wrote poetry. He should sweep streets so well that all the hosts of heaven and earth will pause to say, here lived a great streetsweeper who did his job well.

To paraphrase: if a man is called to work on a ladder, he should climb that ladder even as Richard Branson flew planes, as Bill Gates made software, or as James Dyson created the bagless vacuum cleaner. He should climb his ladder so well that all the hosts of heaven and earth will pause to say, here lived a great Planet Ladder citizen who did his job well.

One way we can help families cope is to get them to understand where their entrepreneurial loved ones are coming from.

Case Study

Lisa accompanied her aspiring entrepreneurial husband to my seminar, which was one of a series of "Start Your Own Business" sessions. She had not attended any of the other sessions, and had decided to sit in only at the last minute.

She sat quietly through the evening, and came up to speak to me as everyone was getting ready to go home.

"I don't think you're being fair to the spouses of would-be entrepreneurs," she said.

"How come?" I replied.

"Because I learned more about what makes my husband tick from you in one hour this evening, than I learned from him in the two years he's been talking about this."

Lisa continued: "Why isn't it compulsory for all partners to attend your "Start Your Own Business" session together with their entrepreneurial loved ones? That way, there will be a lot less unhappy families".

If Lisa is right – and naturally, I think she is – many partners could benefit enormously from learning about the entrepreneurial thought process.

A better understanding of Planet DoingItMyWay can be very therapeutic and comforting for families, especially when they discover that the situation they find themselves in is not unique to them.

Suddenly, they can talk about a subject that was taboo until now.

Suddenly they don't have to feel so bad that their initial reaction to the entrepreneurial announcement was not enthusiastic.

Suddenly, they see that others too fail to rejoice at the prospect of their loved ones deserting Planet Ladder.

And suddenly, they see that entrepreneurial bug can also strike in other normal Planet Ladder families.

In a previous chapter, we suggested that a major source of encouragement for entrepreneurs is other entrepreneurs.

Why not replicate this advice for families?

What happens at present is that, when families are forced to confront the crisis caused by someone in their midst going off the rails and threatening to start their own business, they naturally turn to other Planet Ladder citizens for reassurance.

When this happens, we can be sure of one outcome: these friends will deliver the goods, reinforce Planet Ladder values, and further fuel the fears and anxieties that the family already feel.

A more constructive alternative would be for families to seek advice from other families who are going through the same process. Families would get a more balanced picture if they were to ask other families in the same situation how they coped, what trade-off they negotiated, and what tips they can offer on how to live with an entrepreneur.

Earlier, when we introduced the concept of Entreprenese, we identified some of the phrases that would-be Planet DoingItMyWay citizens seem to pick up with remarkable ease as soon as they embark on the entrepreneurial path.

But what happens when their Planet Ladder families hear these phrases? They hear something *very* different.

You say ...	They hear ...
I'm not comfortable working within an organisation.	I am an anarchist at heart.
I wasn't cut out to bide my time and work my way up the ladder.	I don't have the patience to wait until I am promoted, I want instant gratification NOW.
I know I can make a go of it on my own.	I have an unrealistic belief in myself.
I have fire in the belly.	I've got a bee in my bonnet.
I have passion.	I get myself all worked up over ridiculous notions.
I have vision.	I am delusional.
I have energy.	I'm frustrated.
I am motivated.	Someone has given me a brilliant idea.
I see potential where others see disaster.	I am a fool, rushing in where angels fear to tread.
I see solutions where others think it can't be done.	I believe I can fix anything.
I have the chutzpah to believe I can make it on my own.	I have notions above my station.
I have the chutzpah to embark on a new venture with no guarantee that it will succeed.	I am prepared to take risks at my family's expense.
I have the chutzpah to compete with established companies in my field.	I'm Superman
I have a strong need to be independent.	I hate authority.
I am defined by my need for freedom.	I want to leave you all.

You say ...	They hear ...
I don't like being told what to do.	Stop bugging me.
I want to be a participant, not an observer.	I love philosophising.
I have belief in myself and in what I am trying to create.	I am an over-confident and arrogant so-and-so.
I prefer to rely on myself than on anyone else.	I don't trust you.
I don't waste time wondering whether I did the right thing.	I am never wrong.
I don't like sitting around waiting for things to happen.	I want to be seen as a leader.
I have a long-term perspective.	Don't bother me with little details such as "What will we eat tomorrow?"
I allow my imagination to take me on fascinating journeys.	I'm a dreamer.
I am willing to bend the rules, to be different.	I'm basically dishonest.
I believe in listening to my instincts.	Don't confuse me with the facts.
I am prepared to live with a degree of uncertainty.	I don't care whether you can cope.
I thrive in an unstructured environment.	The family ties me down.
I am not devastated by failure.	I have a death wish.
I'm prepared to work round the clock to get something done.	I'm a boaster.
I'm prepared to forgo a social life while I'm getting my business up and running.	I'll leave you to run the house for a while.

In this chapter, we attempted to redress the balance by looking at ways in which families can achieve a better understanding of their entrepreneurial partners.

At the end of the day, most families must find an equilibrium, which will be reached faster if both parties — Planet Ladder and Planet DoingItMyWay citizens alike – understand the wider story.

This book started with a story of the Three Bears, which painted an idyllic picture of what happens when one member of the family wants to share his or her entrepreneurial news with the family.

We described the on-tap family support depicted in the story as wishful thinking, as a dangerous myth that creates unreasonable expectations on both sides of the divide.

In later chapters we discussed some of the reasons why this myth has become so embedded in the public psyche, and we offered some strategies for coping with the fall-out from the widespread unavailability of on-tap support.

In the final chapter, we will revisit the Three Bears story, and offer a post-revisionist version that is closer to reality.

Chapter 11
The Three Bears Revisited
A Post-Modernist Version of the Classic Fairy Tale

Once upon a time, in a place called Honeytown, there lived three bears: Mummy Bear, Daddy Bear and Baby Bear.

Mummy Bear was a supervisor at the Honeytown Glass Jar Company, where both her parents had also worked before they retired. Mummy Bear liked her job. Ever since she was at school she had wanted a responsible position with a solid employer. Her job at the glass jar plant gave her a sense of security, and she felt very grounded as a contented employee.

Daddy Bear also had a good job. He worked as a security guard in the local branch of First National Honey Bank.

Baby Bear was minded by Grandma Bear.

Daddy Bear was very good at his job. He frequently made suggestions to management on how they could tighten up security at the bank.

He also harboured an entrepreneurial bee in his bonnet. From the time he was in high school, Daddy Bear had toyed with the idea of being his own boss. He didn't yet know in what field he would create his entrepreneurial venture, but he was forever on the lookout for a suitable opportunity.

One day as he was browsing through the Honeytown Times, *Daddy Bear read a report that because of the growing prosperity of Honeytown, three new banks —Bruin Bank, Paddington Bank and Rupert Bank – were all planning to open branches in the town in the near future.*

Daddy Bear's entrepreneurial wheels started turning.

"Now here is a chance for me", he thought to himself.

"I have become extremely knowledgeable in the area of bank security. I've always wanted to do my own thing. Why don't I use my expertise and experience, and set up my own bank security consultancy business, offering my services to the new banks?"

The more Daddy Bear thought about it, the more the idea excited him. However, before rushing off to share his plans with Mummy Bear, he decided to do some reality testing. He went to his boss, and discreetly asked her how she felt about his entrepreneurial plans. She indicated that she would be happy for the bank to call on Daddy Bear's professional expertise if he became a bank security consultant.

Daddy Bear used the opportunity to enquire how much start-up capital his own bank would be willing to make available for the new venture.

He also made tentative enquiries with some colleagues in Bruin Bank, Paddington Bank and Rupert Bank, and asked them to sound out his idea with the decision-makers there.

Only when he had received an enthusiastic endorsement from other friends in business did Daddy Bear decide it was time to inform Mummy Bear of his plans.

Knowing that this would not be easy for her, Daddy Bear deliberately downplayed his enthusiasm and his excitement. He decided to adopt a more subtle and conciliatory approach. He prepared himself mentally for receiving less than a rapturous response to his entrepreneurial announcement. By doing his homework in advance, he tried to have ready answers to counter any fears that Mummy Bear might express.

Daddy Bear also carefully chose the right time and place to tell Mummy Bear. He arranged for a cub-sitter for Baby Bear, and took Mummy Bear out for a meal to her favourite restaurant. As they sipped their honey tea after a very pleasant meal, Daddy Bear said:

"Honeybunch, you know that I'm really good at my job. You know how frequently my suggestions are used by the management of First National Honey Bank to tighten up security at the bank. You have probably guessed that I have always dreamed of having my own business. Well, I've given it a lot of thought, and I believe I now have enough knowledge, experience and contacts to start my own bank security consultancy business.

"Now, I know that this idea of mine will probably worry you. The thought of my leaving my job in the bank to become my own boss will probably frighten you. I can understand that. Your family have always been wage-earners, and you're really not familiar with the world of business. But I've already looked carefully into the whole subject, and I'm sure I can make a success of it. My own boss has indicated that she will be happy to engage me as a consultant. She also said I'd have no problem raising start-up funding. And I have already received assurances from the three new banks coming into town that they too will use my services. So what do you say?"

Mummy Bear reached out and held Daddy Bear's hand.

"Sweetie", she said. "Thank you for being so understanding. Thank you for acknowledging that I would have my doubts about all this. I've become comfortably used to the idea of your salary from the bank coming in every month like clockwork. But I can see how much this means to you, I can see how determined you are, and I can see that you've done a lot of planning. I don't pretend to understand the world of business, but I will honestly try and get used to the idea. I must admit that I didn't realise just how much drive, ambition and initiative you had in you."

"Honeybunch," replied Daddy Bear, "it is I who should be thanking you. I've heard of so many bears who were given a terrible time by their wives when they announced that they wanted to start their own business."

"I don't promise that I will always be patient or tolerant about all this," said Mummy Bear, "but I will try and be as supportive as I can."

The next evening, Mummy Bear organised an impromptu get-together for all the family to tell them about Daddy Bear's plans.

Grandpa Bear frowned as he growled: "I hope you know what you're doing, son".

Daddy Bear's brother, Bruno, asked whether First National Honeybank would take him back if the business didn't succeed.

Cousin Beryl Bear sobbed into her handkerchief, as she saw visions of Daddy Bear standing in the line for social security after his business venture had folded.

Mummy Bear put on a brave face. She was still anxious, she still was not delighted at Daddy Bear's decision, but she loved him enough to trust his judgement.

All in all, Daddy Bear was pleased with the way he had handled his entrepreneurial announcement.

He also thought that Mummy Bear and the rest of the family had reacted better than he dared hope. He knew that they didn't quite understand what was driving his entrepreneurial motor, but he also knew that they wished him well.

Daddy Bear gave in his notice at First National Honey Bank. He took out a loan from his former employer, and opened a small office in downtown Honeytown.

First National Honey Bank became his first customer. When Bruin Bank, Paddington Bank and Rupert Bank came to town, they all engaged Daddy Bear as a consultant. Within a year, Daddy Bear's company was supplying security services to all the banks in Honeytown and beyond.

As time passed, Mummy Bear's anxiety level fell. She saw that Daddy Bear was doing well, and that he was happy running his own business. She saw that their income had not changed noticeably, and was even growing slowly. She began to take more interest in the business, and even started thinking that Baby Bear might one day join Daddy Bear.

Daddy Bear, Mummy Bear and Baby Bear all lived happily ever after.

The End.

About the Author

Yanky Fachler is a "Start Your Own Business" consultant, speaker, author and trainer, as well as a freelance writer specialising in brochures, websites and other promotional material.

Born in the UK, Yanky earned his BA and MA from Brunel University, and worked as management consultant in Israel before setting up his own advertising copywriting agency in the 1980s. At the same time, he began a parallel career on the amateur stage and founded Israel's national amateur drama association. For several years, Yanky served on the executive board of the International Amateur Theatre Association based in Tallinn, Estonia.

After succumbing to the charms of an Irish lass at an international drama festival, Yanky eventually moved to Ireland in 1998, and established BallyHoo Entrepreneurial Consulting as a vehicle for his popular "Start Your Own Business" seminars and workshops.

His first book was *Fire in the Belly: An Exploration of the Entrepreneurial Spirit*, which tackles the neglected issue of how to make the emotional transition from employee to self-employed.

Yanky conducts training workshops throughout Ireland, and frequently travels to the USA to address conferences and seminars. In Ireland, he often serves as a media spokesman on the subject of "Start Your Own Business".

Yanky's Entrepreneurial Seminars

Whether he is addressing a small seminar or a conference audience of hundreds, Yanky (usually accompanied by his ubiquitous ladder) adopts a distinctive and entertaining motivational style that brings his subject alive. Yanky's seminars include:

DO I HAVE WHAT IT TAKES TO BE MY OWN BOSS?
Targeted at people who are thinking of starting their own business, this workshop gives valuable insight into the entrepreneurial experience, helping participants understand the emotional transition from the world of employment to the world of self employment.

IS LOSING YOUR JOB A GOOD REASON FOR STARTING YOUR OWN BUSINESS?
Redundancy can often be seen as the opportunity to go and start a business. This workshop helps people who have already lost their job or could lose their job to explore self-employment as an option, and to discover whether anger is a sufficient trigger for starting a business.

EXPLODING THE MYTH OF ON-TAP EMOTIONAL SUPPORT
It is a myth that people shouldn't even consider starting a business unless their family wholeheartedly supports the decision. This workshop explores why the very people from whom budding entrepreneurs crave support are unable to give it, and offers tips on how spouses and partners can better understand where their entrepreneurial partners are coming from.

WHATEVER POSSESSED ME TO BE MY OWN BOSS?
Many people running their own businesses feel jaded, overworked and under appreciated. Above all, they feel lonely. They forget why they wanted to be their own boss in the first place. This workshop helps to re-motivate, re-energise and inspire owner managers of small and medium businesses.

ALL YOU NEED IS CHUTZPAH
Targeted at people who are starting their own business and at those who are part of a larger organisation, this workshop explores how to use chutzpah - a combination of nerve, bottle, cheek, gall and balls - to forge ahead of the pack.

ALSO BY YANKY FACHLER

Fire in the Belly: An Exploration of the Entrepreneurial Spirit

In this take-no-prisoners approach to entrepreneurship, Yanky Fachler shows that the key ingredient to success in starting your own business is not what you have to do but who you have to be. He outlines the thrill, the challenge, the fun and the problems of going it alone, and offers tips on what to watch out for.

This highly accessible book is packed with case studies and anecdotes. Yanky itemises the prerequisites for entrepreneurship, and explores the different mindset and different culture between the world of employment and the world of self-employment.

The author concludes that, with fire in the belly, anyone will be able to master the entrepreneurial skills.

Praise for *Fire in the Belly*

Your book is so motivational, and answered so many things I have been wondering about myself for years. I will also highly recommend the book to others, and I certainly hope they enjoy it as much as I did. **Nuala Acton, Director, Eventime, Ireland**

You don't often find a book that walks you through things like the pros and cons of entrepreneurship. I really enjoyed it, the tone is light and easy to read. If you are seriously considering becoming your own boss, the book does a very good job in making you think about the decision to go it alone - before you jump in up to your neck. **Deiric McCann, Cara, Aer Lingus magazine**

When I first picked up your book, I realised that every page was talking directly to me. I found myself nodding in agreement on every page. Your book emboldened me to find the courage to start my own business. I keep it with me at all times, dipping into its chapters for advice, encouragement and inspiration. **Ciara Mullen, Founder of e-nails Nail Bar**

OAK TREE PRESS

Ireland's leading business book publisher,
Oak Tree Press is increasingly an international developer
and publisher of enterprise training and support solutions.

Oak Tree Press has developed "platforms" of
Pre-start-up, Start-up, Growth and Support content,
which include publications, websites, software,
assessment models, training, consultancy and certification.

Oak Tree Press' enterprise training and support solutions
are in use in Ireland, the UK, USA, Scandinavia and Eastern Europe
and are available for customisation to local situations and needs.

For further information, contact:
Ron Immink or Brian O'Kane.
OAK TREE PRESS
19 Rutland Street, Cork, Ireland
T: + 353 21 431 3855   F: + 353 21 431 3496
E: info@oaktreepress.com
W: www.oaktreepress.com

www.oaktreepress.com